DROESE RANEY X DESIGN

MSP-10

DROESE RANEY X DESIGN

WRITTEN WITH IAN VOLNER

ORO EDITIONS | ANDREA MONFRIED EDITIONS

ORO Editions
Publishers of Architecture, Art, and Design
Gordon Goff: Publisher
www.oroeditions.com
info@oroeditions.com

Andrea Monfried Editions
www.andreamonfried.com

Published by ORO Editions and Andrea Monfried Editions.

Book Design: Julie Savasky, Overstory Design
Project Manager: Jake Anderson
Prepress: Professional Graphics, Inc.
Printing: ORO Group Inc.

Printed in China

10 9 8 7 6 5 4 3 2 1 First Edition

Library of Congress Control Number: 2023938960
ISBN: 978-1-957183-81-7

ORO Editions makes a continuous effort to minimize the overall carbon footprint of its publications. As part of this goal, ORO, in association with Global ReLeaf, arranges to plant trees to replace those used in the manufacturing of the paper produced for its books. Global ReLeaf is an international campaign run by American Forests, one of the world's oldest nonprofit conservation organizations. Global ReLeaf is American Forests' education and action program that helps individuals, organizations, agencies, and corporations improve the local and global environment by planting and caring for trees.

ADDITIONAL CREDITS
PAGE 418: Chandra North photographed by Fredrik Brodén for B, the magazine of Briggs Freeman Sotheby's International Realty. Stylist: Stephanie Quadri. Hair and makeup artist: Michael Thomas. Producer: Rob Brinkley
THE EXTRA MILE cover: Valerie Chang
TEN TIMES OVER cover: Sansho Scott / BFA.com
FRIENDS AND FAMILY cover: Maj Lindstrom
THIS IS THE WAY cover: Blake Wright

COVER MURAL

'Untitled' 2016

ARTIST
Huy Nguyen

MEDIUM
Wall Mural at
2800 Main (18' x 116')

COMMISSIONED BY
Westdale Real
Estate Management
and Droese Raney

PHOTO OF MURAL ON
COVER BY FREDRIK BRODEN

CONTENTS

DROESE
ITECTURE,
FIRE ZONE
AMB. 224
FIRE 244
ST AID

← FLIGHT DIRECTION →
FRAGILE
US - 3365
HT

Creating this book has reminded me just how lucky I am. Lucky to be doing what I've always wanted to do; lucky to be doing it with the great collaborators who appear in these pages; and lucky to be doing it with my best friend and business partner, Lance Raney. I share memories of late nights in New York, Guadalajara, and around the world with him and with our Droese Raney family, the team members who've shared our firm's vision and made every day a fun day.

None of this luck would have been possible without my actual family. My wife, Suzanne, has been my biggest cheerleader since the early days of Droese Architecture, making it possible for me to maintain my own practice. My mother and sisters have always supported me along my path. And finally, my two sons, Will and Henry, surprise and inspire me at every turn. Seeing this world through your eyes makes life so much sweeter. —**DD**

This book is for my parents, who encouraged and supported my dreams; for my wife, who stuck by my side; and for my two boys, who inspire me every day. —**LR**

FORTY FIVE TEN

DESIGN X BASICS

Plainspoken eloquence may sound like a contradiction in terms. But in these three projects, Droese Raney gets to the point with style to spare.

It's hard to be simple. Among other things, there's no broad agreement as to what simple even means, as regards architecture and design anyway. In the 1930s, practitioners of Art Deco regarded their stylistics as hard-boiled and stripped-down; twenty years later, Deco appeared positively gaudy, at least compared to the astringency of the International Style; and twenty years after that, Brutalism made the Seagram Building look as lavish and bedizened as a rhinestone. Excess, as well as restraint, is in the eye of the beholder and as prone to changing times and tastes as anything else.

Anything to do with aesthetics, that is. Beyond what the eye can see, there might be another way to talk about simplicity in the design field, a model somewhat more stable and substantial. Many in the field have extolled the virtues of basicness as a conceptual tool—the whole notion of the *parti*, going back to the Beaux-Arts, demands reducing a project to its essentials and then building outward. Others see simplicity as something, well, simpler: a mode; a disposition; not a style of architecture, but a style of architect. Rare in a profession dominated by the uptight and the overpolished, such practices are possessed of a casualness and self-assurance that imbues everything they do with an air of ease.

Of course, it takes just the right project to bring those qualities to the fore—and fortunately for Droese Raney, that project has come along over and over for nearly a quarter century. Ever since David Droese and Lance Raney set up shop in Dallas in 1998, the architects have steadily expanded their range, moving from commercial interiors to multiuse ground-up developments and beyond, all while maintaining a feeling for fundamentals that seems an organic extension of their individual personae. Born and raised in Ohio (Droese) and Texas (Raney), the two met as undergrads at Texas Tech University and discovered that they shared a view of architecture as being co-material with the everyday experience of their lives: the rugged southwestern landscape; tearing through it on the back of a souped-up motorcycle; stopping for chips and *queso* and then heading back into town to hit up a gallery opening. The undeniable appeal of this outlook has drawn an array of likeminded collaborators, swelling the office's ranks with exceptional designers, while also attracting exceptional clients.

Perhaps nothing in the firm's portfolio demonstrates their elemental attitude more perfectly than their Manhattan location for fashion brand **BILLY REID**. Known for his scruffy yet tasteful, formally informal approach to men's and women's apparel, the eponymous designer has made his hometown of Florence, Alabama, an unlikely sartorial capital, the center of a sprawling empire with retail locations around the country that caters to style icons from Scarlett Johansson to James Bond. For the New York crowd, Reid turned to Droese Raney to translate his unique take on all-American couture into a suitably tony, but at the same time comfortable environment, one that could make discriminating downtowners feel right at home while transporting them to a realm of laid-back, countrified chic. In an added twist, the architects would have to pull off this challenging double act within the cast-iron frame of one of the East Village's most celebrated buildings, the former Bond Street Savings Bank (later the Bouwerie Lane Theatre), originally constructed in 1874.

The architects responded with a design that turns the space into a paean to cozy authenticity. Visitors enter the double-height interior to find themselves in a kind of spruced-up Collyer's mansion: Persian rugs line the floor, chandeliers dangle from above, and claw-footed chaises and richly upholstered fauteuils create welcoming niches, quiet demispaces that break up the open plan without balkanizing it. Exposed brick lets the historic building speak for itself, only now with a bit of the South in its mouth, its accent altered through the extensive use of reclaimed wood, hunting trophies, and other fixtures culled by the designers (following Reid's suggestions) from salvage sales below the Mason-Dixon. Their most ingenious bit of salvage is also the design's most eye-catching moment—the spindles around the staircase, all pulled from different houses and from different eras and styles, making the journey to the lower level feel like a trip into the past. Once at the bottom, fashion fans can admire the panel-lined ceiling, then take a tumbler of complimentary whiskey and settle into a mellow frame of mind, the preferred mental setting for Droese Raney and Billy Reid alike.

A similar confluence of sensibilities is evident in the firm's work with **NEIGHBORHOOD GOODS**, a retailer that takes the idea of the classic department store and brings it down to earth and into the future. With locations in Dallas, Austin, and New York, the company teams up with small-scale and emerging creators of cutting-edge clothing, cosmetics, and homewares, giving brick-and-mortar space to digital-native brands. Accompanied by low-key in-house drinks and dining, the individual stores are amiable, ever-changing environments where the focus is as much on people as on products. Just the kind of place, in other words, that Droese Raney likes best.

From the instant they cross the threshold, customers at the Dallas location are acclimated to this rarified commercial climate by way of a design language that states the architects' intentions as plainly as possible. Bold, geometric graphics; a modest material palette of wood, polished concrete, and metal; abundant foliage, monsteras and pothos and empire ferns, all sprouting from gleaming white planters and shelving: every aspect of the interior communicates a relaxed, almost domestic chill, with a potent dose of Zen and a hint of social media–friendly cool. Reflecting the store's revolving offerings, the display cases can be shifted and altered for different goods from different neighbors. At the brand's Austin location, the central bar area operates as a display case of its own, its funnel-like serving platform and surrounding stools making an alluring spectacle of the bottles, glasses, and patrons enjoying them. Once again (and again: the company now also boasts a New York location, at Chelsea Market, from Droese Raney), the designers' artful effortlessness shows through.

HATCHWAYS represents a different manifestation of the same impulse—here applied to what would otherwise seem the antithesis of Droese Raney's easygoing ethos. As much as the designers believe in playing around, they also believe in hard work, and their project for the innovative Dallas-based coworking brand shows that they can combine the two for the changing nature of the post-pandemic economy. Part high-tech office, part creative studio, part food-and-beverage hang spot, Hatchways thrived even as similar businesses struggled, a success that owes much to the design of their space in the Victory Park neighborhood. Located just steps from the American Airlines Center, the multiuse interior is a bastion of calm in one of Big D's largest entertainment districts, offering small companies and freelancers the time and tools they need to get things done (as well as plenty of ways to celebrate afterward).

Situated on the first level, the primary office suite features snug, compartmentalized work desks, glassed-in conference lounges, and bubble-like private booths soundproofed against the hustle and bustle of the busy interior and the street life just beyond the floor-to-ceiling windows. Upstairs, smaller bookable rooms afford a more conventional corporate-type atmosphere, while recording studios and tech labs allow users to record podcasts, edit digital films, or conduct video conferences as the need arises. At every turn, the facility presents members and their guests with a mood the company refers to as "friendly futurism," a soft, faintly nostalgic environment of bright colors, soft curves, and cushy materiality that seems to hark back to 60s-era sci-fi. (Note in particular the glamorous—and distinctly Kubrickian—red-tiled bar.) As so often with Droese Raney, the design places a special emphasis on places to take a load off and decompress: its most important public-facing amenity is the airy, health-oriented restaurant and café just adjacent to the entrance. There, as visitors lean into the plush banquette seating, surrounded by crisp white and wood surfaces and under an openwork ceiling, the world seems to come into focus at last, the architects once again bringing everything back to basics.

Billy Reid

Beautiful Music

BILLY REID

My mom had a store growing up—it was in my grandmother's old house. She had this incredible vibe in the store: there was a kitchen in the back, and people would stop by just to hang out. It was literally a house that had this really interesting clothing store in it. I just loved the way that felt, and I said, Man, if I ever have a store, I want it to feel exactly that way. At the time we launched the Soho shop, there was nothing like that, definitely not in New York. The whole menswear scene in the city was kind of lost; everything was really dry, really minimalist-contemporary. What we did helped to change things in a big way. A lot of people jumped on the wagon after that.

I had been lobbying to open the New York store since day one. We had contacts in New York, I had worked in New York, been in the game there. I really felt like that was the place we needed to be. I knew it was going to be expensive, and also hard to find the right spot. We looked for a place for, I don't know, two years. The funny thing is that the first building I went to look at was the one on Bond Street: I could not get that place out of my head. Finally, we came back and said, You know what, let's do it right here on the Bowery, in the old Bouwerie Lane Theatre. The neighborhood felt like it was up and coming, and the space was just incredible, with those high ceilings and everything.

We knew we'd have to make it work with our brand, with our identity. Which is—well, I don't actually have a stock answer for that. We just kind of wing it every time. I guess you could say we're kind of an ageless brand: we make products that live with you and get better as you wear them. But it's so personal to me. The aesthetic, the vibe—it's something we've built and grown, and whatever else it is, personal connectivity is key. We like things with a broken-in feel, with a sense of warmth to them, and we want people to be able to wear these things and use them in very versatile situations. That's the goal. We're based in the South, so we kind of see things through a different lens. Coming from this little town in north Alabama, we're trying to make some beautiful music and hoping people listen.

***Southern charm:** The Reid and Droese Raney collaboration extended to multiple locations, including one on New Orleans's storied Magazine Street.*

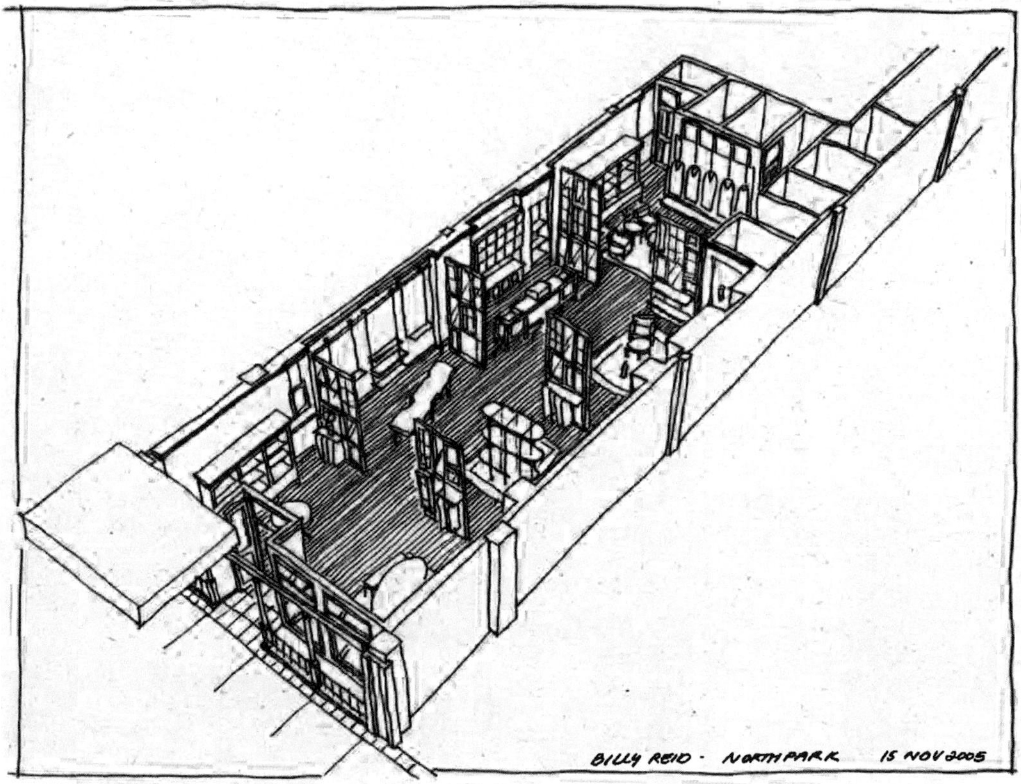

The plan comes together: *As homey and informal as Reid's stores can feel, their spatial dynamics are carefully plotted by the designers, as in the case of the NorthPark location in Dallas.*

Right from the start, it just felt like Droese Raney heard us loud and clear. I knew the firm had this strong background in retail, but really it all happened based on those kinds of personal connections we always believe in. We had mutual friends, and they said, "Hey, we're going to meet with these guys. They do a lot of great work for different folks." I said, "Sure, sounds great, let's go." And we met, had a lot of laughs, talked about a lot of ideas, maybe had a few drinks. I remember bringing a lot of funky pictures and little samples and things. It really evolved into something unique.

Part of it was this shared love of found objects. The whole personal curation process is so important for us, and it turned out the Droese Raney folks were the same way. I knew the firm had done a lot of artisanal collaborations, and I definitely wanted to push them more in that direction. We spent a lot of time actually looking for materials and figuring out how we could use them. Taking reclaimed blocks of wood and making new things out of them; making a cabinet or a table; getting spindles and cutting them to size: the Droese team was so deep into that on every level, and you see all that love of craft and adaptive reuse all over the store. The customized racks, the exposed brick. I love having contrasting textures: that old staircase against those brand-new finishes, clean and beautiful, the white and the wood. It made the whole space come together. It started becoming *us*, and it was because it had that sentimental core to it.

One thing is for sure, that space definitely found an audience. When we first opened up, we held this big block party. We brought some friends of ours from Louisiana—they have this famous old seafood place, and they came and fried fish right out there on the corner, serving it up to magazine editors and people like that. The party was such a hit the police showed up and started to hand out citations. We realized that that might be our first and last Big Apple Street Barbecue—but that didn't stop people from coming to the store. Everybody in the neighborhood would stop by, look in, and ask, "What's going on here?" It was 2008, the stock market had just crashed, but we kept going. People in the fashion scene, people who'd heard of us or seen us in magazines, they would all check out the shop when they were in town. As often as not, they'd stay for a drink, hang out for two or three hours. Before you know it, we're getting all this recognition. The store ended up being a big pivot point for us.

It was only a couple years after that that I got the Menswear Designer of the Year award from CFDA. And we've just grown and grown since. In a sense, when I think about our brand identity, the store really helps define it. It came into focus when Droese Raney came aboard. I don't think it could have happened for a lot of other people in the fashion world, or with a lot of other architects. Business has gotten a lot more complicated these days, and things like this just don't happen off the cuff. Everything takes so much more intention and planning, versus just letting something happen. But you know what I can guaran-damn-tee you? Letting it happen is the best way.

Mood board: *To capture the offbeat essence of the brand, Droese Raney channeled influences and inspiration from the American South, country music, traditional interiors, and hipster chic.*

The buck stops here: *The architects and their client have been known to get into some antics. But the big hunting trophy at the New York store isn't one they bagged themselves: they scored it on a visit to a regional secondhand shop.*

FULTON & ROARK
FULTON & ROARK

BILLY REID

WITH SIGNS FOLLOWING

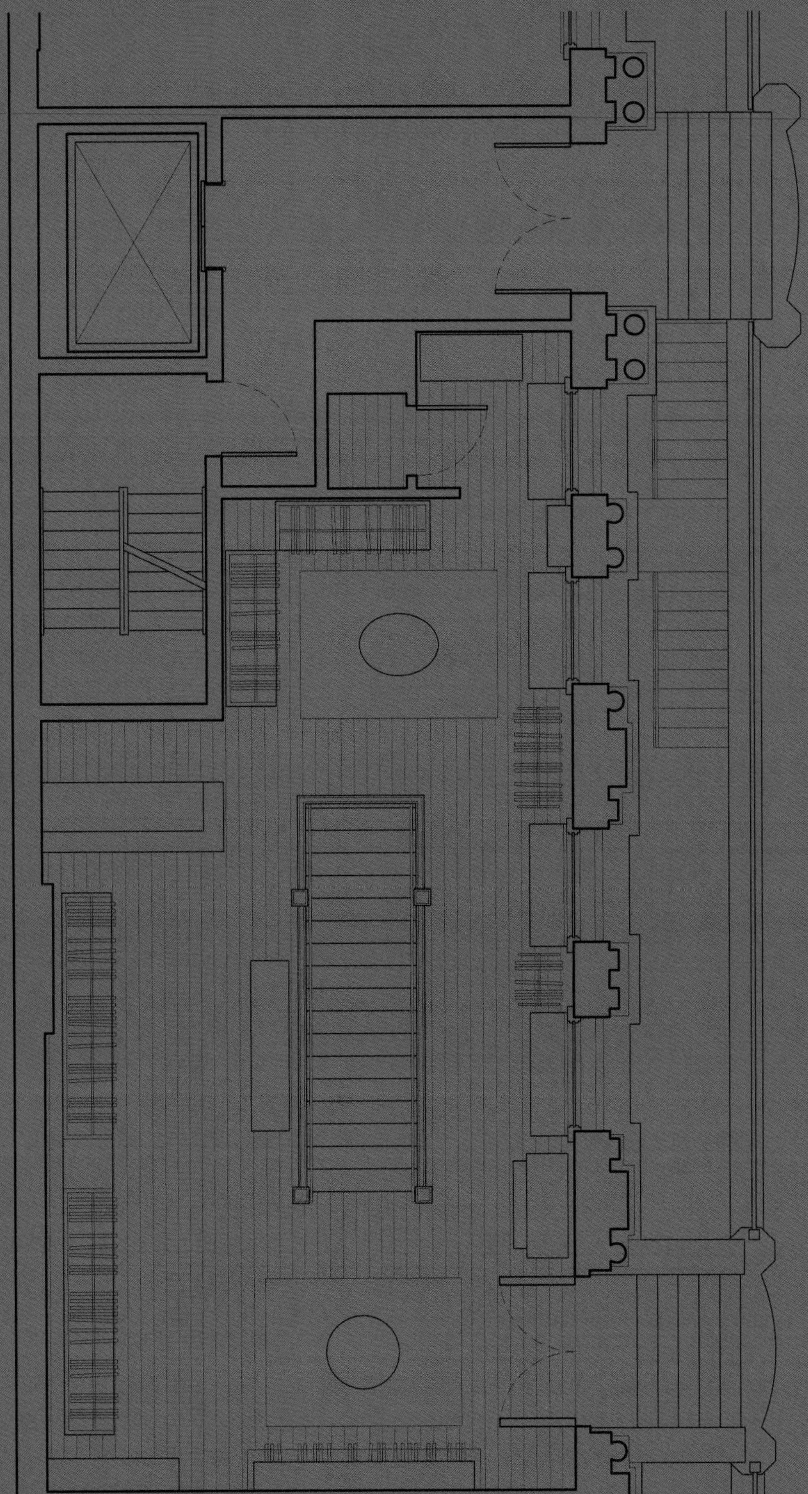

LEVEL 1

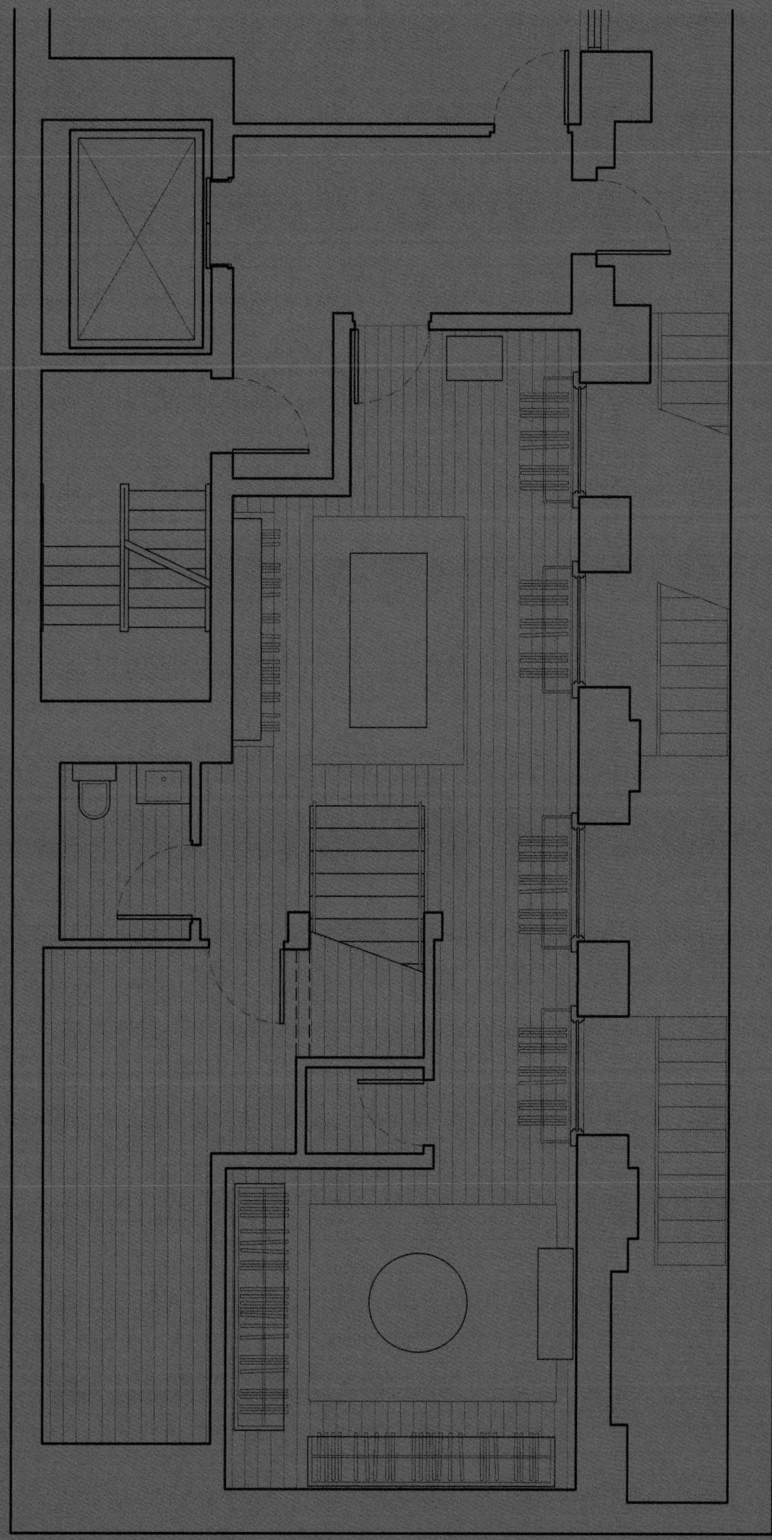

LEVEL 2

MOORE
&
GILES
FULTON & ROARK

EXIT

Neighborhood Goods

Neighborhoo

Goods

SKIN CARE
UpWest
IZIPIZI

Prim and Proper
Prim and Proper
NOW FEATURING
ADULT GRILLED CHEESE
&
TORTILLA SOUP
COFFEE TEA
ESPRESSO & PASTRIES
APPS SOUP SALADS
& SANDWICHES
COCKTAILS
WINE & BEER
HAPPY HOUR M-F 4–7

THOUSAND FELL
TONAL
The Smartest Home Gym
RAINS

EAT SOME FOOD!

CARBON
Neighborhood
Goods

CHEN
TASCHEN
40 TASCHEN SINCE 1980
FORMGIVING
Nomadic HOMES
STAN LEE'S STORY
CHAGALL
Dalí TAROT
DALI The Paintings
STEVE McCURRY ANIMALS
On YOGA
SURFING
Architecture in the 20th Century
GOODS GIFTS
ADIDAS ARCHIVE
bauhaus
James Baldwin
Steve Schapiro
The Fire Next Time
20th Century Photography
THE POLAROID BOOK
THE GRAND TOUR
AI WEIWEI
PHOTO ICONS
EGON SCHIELE

Aēsop.
Departure
Arrival
STATES OF BEING: AROMATIQUE ROOM SPRAY TRIO
Body Cleansing Slab

CUTS
Classic Curve

Split Hem

YOGA
TASCHEN

EXIT
PERSONAL CARE

SKIN CARE

Hatchways

How Can it Disrupt

The Range
vintage trailer resort

Hatchways
POD
A

DESIGN X PROGRESS

On the Dallas homefront, two adaptive reuse projects see the architects take on the unique history of the city and embrace its diverse community.

Droese Raney's development has been guided less by a series of fixed principles than by an intuitive sense for design's potential to effect change. In this regard, the office's location has been a distinct asset—since the partners started out in Dallas twenty-five years ago, the north Texas metropole has changed dramatically, and its ever-shifting social, economic, and physical character is at once reflected in and influenced by the firm's evolving work. Even as the architects' theater of operations has expanded as far as Colorado, California, New York, and beyond, their hometown has continued to play a key role in their growth, rivaled by perhaps only one other factor: the arrival of their associates (now vice presidents) Christine Howitt and Reid Mulligan.

With the addition of the two designers—both hailing from Dallas—the practice has been able not only to lengthen its reach but to greatly widen its purview, designing everything from minute custom fixtures to urban-scale projects of startling logistical complexity. Rounding out Raney's and Droese's particular strengths, Mulligan and Howitt also complement their shared temperament, the generational difference between them adding a bit of Millennial intensity to the office's native Gen X cool. The singular combination of sensibilities and technical expertise was key to creating two of the office's most significant, change-making contributions to the Dallas landscape.

Taking its name from its location at the corner of Elm Street and the Good Latimer Expressway, GOOD E is a multistructural compound at the outermost edge of one of Dallas's most celebrated historic districts. Beginning in the 1910s, Deep Ellum (a Texasization of *Deep Elm*) was a major hub of Dallas's vibrant industrial economy, packed with manufacturing plants and auto showrooms; at the same time, it served as a center of business and civic life for the city's thriving African American community—at least until the advent of the highway system, which tore through the area's urban fabric after midcentury and turned it into a largely vacant slum. Only since about 1990 has Deep Ellum begun to return to life, becoming a favored spot for music and arts venues, many of them dedicated to the rich cultural legacy of the prewar years, back when it was the regular haunt of legendary performers like Bessie Smith and Lead Belly. Droese Raney's project continues the process of historical healing and brings a new verve to the old neighborhood.

Four extant commercial facades, built as retail storefronts in the early twentieth century, have been carefully restored and connected to form an original ensemble. An added structure launches over the three westerly volumes and settles down next to the fourth. Home to a vast, open-plan office space, the rooftop component affords dramatic views over the neighborhood while giving visitors a glimpse to the area's workaday past through the exposed brick walls of the adjacent commercial buildings, some with half-faded advertising murals still visible. The language of the new construction distinguishes itself from the old through its echt-modernist, black-steel framing and broad expanses of glass, while the deft planar and sectional scheme provides for a courtyard garden at the heart of the complex, a moment of calm and reflection in a neighborhood that once again teems with activity.

Only a few blocks away, **2800 MAIN** is the address of an equally ambitious intervention, this one spanning an entire block between North Crowdus Street and Malcolm X Boulevard. Here the challenge was even more difficult: to create a coherent, welcoming commercial and entertainment zone from a jumbled collection of long disused buildings and empty lots while at the same time preserving the hard-edged character of the site. Once again, the Droese Raney solution shows what they can do when given room to run.

This time, two upper-story annexes top the low-rise structures—only here the new volumes hide somewhat discreetly just above the historic cornice line, providing rooftop outdoor spaces for the food and beverage establishments within. The eastern addition makes its presence felt only on the Malcolm X side, where it meets the public with a strong, black-clad facade that acts as a gateway to the development. The procession it inaugurates is another journey into the past: guests snake through the interior of the block, following paths from store to store (including the Harlow Bar and Restaurant, its interior also by Droese Raney); back outside, they pass the flanks of the vintage industrial buildings around them. At the very center, visitors find yet another surprising moment of tranquility: a central open space bound by pockmarked brick walls, perhaps an invitation to reflect on the history of the area and the history of the city.

For Dallasites, Droese Raney's transformation of Deep Ellum represents a powerful example of what their city can be: an open, authentically urban environment, with an indelible connection to its own cultural heritage. For the architects, it's only further proof of their extraordinary well of talent, and of their commitment to pushing design—and their community—forward.

Good E

BUY

VELVET TACO
OPEN REALLY LATE
TACOS WITHOUT BORDERS

THE
PERFECT
SODA
only

1910
2550

GOOD
E

EXIT

J.D. SMITH
1910
19 J.D. SMITH 10

THE
SODA

Self Storage
Elm
2600
2500
HC
VELVET TACO
TACOS WITHOUT

Good-Latimer
100
200

2800 Main

2823

HARLOWE
2823

M
M

EXI

042
048
049
053
054
055
059
060
061

PARTS - SERVICE

EXIT
EXIT

EXIT

EXIT

Elm
2900
2800
IdleRye
IdleRye

ONI
RAMEN
HIDE
DEEP
ELLUM
ANY
TIME
Ma
100
OPEN

DESIGN X DESIRE

In a profession plagued by over-seriousness, the firm breaks the mold, bringing the pleasure principle back into the built environment.

Gaston Bachelard knew a thing or two about architecture. The name of the French *philosophe* gets trotted out pretty regularly in design discourse, usually in connection with his most famous book, *The Poetics of Space*, a learned and lyrical meditation on place, memory, and the meaning of home. But his architectural admirers may find themselves alarmed on opening one of his other, no less influential works, *The Psychoanalysis of Fire*. Besides the fact that its subject is inimical to buildings as such, it contains the following passage:

> It is always . . . through a kind of extra pleasure—like dessert—that fire shows itself a friend of man. It does not confine itself to cooking; it makes things crisp and crunchy, it puts the golden crust on the griddle cake . . . As far back in time as we can go, the gastronomic value has always been more highly prized than the nutritive value, and it is in joy and not in sorrow that man discovered his intellect. The conquest of the superfluous gives us a greater spiritual excitement than the conquest of necessity.

Without in any way meaning to, the author is throwing down a gauntlet to the design profession as a whole. The field stakes its chief cultural claim on its own supposed primacy: on the idea that, before we do anything else, we have to have a roof over our heads. If Bachelard is right—if cupidity is the true mother of invention—that means there are human impulses antecedent to, and maybe more important than, the demand for mere shelter. It is a notion most displeasing to architects' ears, and most of them would squirm at the suggestion.

But then Droese Raney is not most architects.

The Dallas-based crew is clearly comfortable with some of those essential non-essentials that old Gaston was talking about—the kind that can turn a space from sufficient to scintillating, from rice crackers to coconut-glazed Thai *khao neeo mamuang*. Though varying wildly in both function and form, the three projects in this section all demonstrate a keen appreciation for a range of emotive categories frequently left out of architecture's affective remit. Acquisitiveness; appetite; plain, undisguised covetousness: embracing these sentiments, the Texans thumb their noses at the discipline's quasi-official anhedonia, winding up the squares in a way that recalls another great philosopher, speaking of his religious upbringing in New York. "'*Wanna'* was a sin all by itself!" said George Carlin. "Thou Shalt Not *Wanna*." Droese Raney not only knows what people want, but that they want to want.

Case in point: the FORTY FIVE TEN flagship store. Conceived by local retail magnate Brian Bolke, the 37,000-square-foot space near the corner of Main and North Ervay Street did not, on its completion in 2016, seem to augur great things. Except for the historic Neiman Marcus headquarters directly across the street from Forty Five Ten, Downtown was a neglected sea of mostly empty parking spots; a small band of intrepid developers (most prominently local entrepreneur Tim Headington) had begun to make inroads in the area, but their efforts were still years from fruition. To realize Bolke's ambition, Droese Raney would have to somehow create a ground-up, four-story temple of style, summoning from the urban ether a vision of elegance.

Inside a simple, vaguely historicist brick envelope, enlivened by a glowing marquee and glazed upper-level dining terrace, the architects carved out a suite of spaces on a simple symmetrical plan. With the individual modules acting as "pavilions," the store gives each category or brand its own identity, its own feeling of secluded privilege; the airy space between the pavilions and the double-height ceilings gives the interior the glamorous appeal of a Manhattan loft. Even more seductive is the material palette, the patterned stone, light bronze, and elaborate tilework (some of it sourced from Droese Raney's longtime collaborators in Guadalajara, Mexico) that create a dazzling ornamental effect. The marble-fronted entryways; the wrought window grills; and perhaps most of all, the use throughout of signature furniture, window, and floor treatments from the classic Knoll catalogue—selected through a close collaboration with the famous design company—make the building read exactly as intended: as a jewel box of many drawers, each lined with delicate stuff and packed with goodies.

Along with its adjacent green space, now an icon of the area (designed by Hocker with Droese Raney consulting), Forty Five Ten touched off a renaissance for Downtown Dallas that is still underway today. New bars, new restaurants, and new cultural destinations have followed in its wake, and the store continues to be a linchpin of the now-thriving neighborhood. Giving Dallasites exactly what they craved, the project also gave them a change they didn't know they needed.

Droese Raney's penchant for conspicuous yet tasteful consumption gets another workout in THE WAREHOUSE. Located in an unassuming corner of North Dallas, the former industrial space–turned–art facility holds the 800-item Rachofsky Collection of paintings, sculpture, and installations in a simple, 31,000-square-foot enclosure. Leaving the raw simplicity of the existing structure intact, the architects transformed the interior into an open-storage treasure house for contemporary art.

Working alongside client and renowned art collector Howard Rachofsky, Droese Raney produced an environment that lets the collector's singular curatorial instincts take center stage. The designers' interventions—painting the exterior a neutral gray; erecting simple white partition walls; revealing the spare white space-frame above, topped by skylights and exposed mechanicals—all take a step back, allowing the displayed work to provide the spatial action as it zooms in scale from the mammoth to the intimate, from a towering sculpture to a tiny still life. Even at the moment of highest architectural drama, in the cozy library-lounge with its built-in bookshelves, the renovation keeps the emphasis on Rachofsky's cultural mission, with concealed shelf lighting (a feature about which the client expressed some initial misgivings) giving the staid catalogues a kind of totemic allure. As the concentrated expression of one individual's lifelong passion for artistic possession, the project is a celebration of finding and getting: a monument to beautiful things, to the desire for more of them, and to desire itself.

Two years after their initial collaboration, Droese Raney and Brian Bolke joined up again, building on their legacy with another somewhat improbable success. The client-designer duo's sequel to Forty Five Ten, THE CONSERVATORY is a 7,000-square-foot boutique opened in 2019 and featuring a comparable lineup of carefully curated clothing, fragrances, objets d'art, and more, demonstrating once again Bolke's unique eye for understated luxury. The primary difference is the locale: though he would subsequently open another Droese Raney–designed space in Dallas's Highland Park Village, Bolke opted to launch his new enterprise in New York City, at the very center of America's fashion universe.

For the architects, the change in venue was made the more daunting by the immediate context—the Hudson Yards megamall on Manhattan's West Side, not yet completed at the time but racing toward its high-profile debut. Working against the clock, in a limited space, and cheek by jowl with dozens of international brands and other architects, Droese Raney crafted a solution that surprises the visitor with its quiet, rustic minimalism, living up to the conceit of the name with a pair of greenhouse-like framed structures inserted directly behind the storefront; a third projects outward from the central entrance bay. Polished flagstone floors are complemented by distinctly midcenturyish steel display cases, a whiff of nostalgia kept in check by the decidedly contemporary lighting scheme with its gridiron track hanging above. A little bit country, a little bit rock 'n' roll, the Conservatory steps lightly into the manic fray that is Hudson Yards, drawing in the city folk with an irresistible image of casual cool.

Forty Five Ten

FORTY

E TEN
THE WILSON
APARTMENT HOMES

SERGE LUTENS

(MALIN+GOETZ)

LE LABO®
GRASSE – NEW YORK
Freshly handmade fine fragrances right at Forty Five Ten's doorstep…
in Downtown Dallas. In order to guarantee the freshness of your creation,
Le Labo has opened a lab across Main Street, where your fragrance
and candle is hand-prepared to order, and personalized.
It will be hand-delivered to you at Forty Five Ten
in less than 10 minutes – just the time you need to grab that pair
of stilettos or perfect leather jacket!
You ARE very welcome!
Le Labo at Forty Five Ten

FOR
HER

COMME
DES GARCONS

SANDER

Berlut

OAMC

LOVED

ALAÏA

Elizabeth
Taylor

JEWELRY
FASHION
GAIA
REFLECTIONS
REFLECTIONS
REFLECTIONS
OTTOMAN CHIC
THE LIGHT OF VENICE
THE LIGHT OF ISTANBUL

ASSOULINE

T F

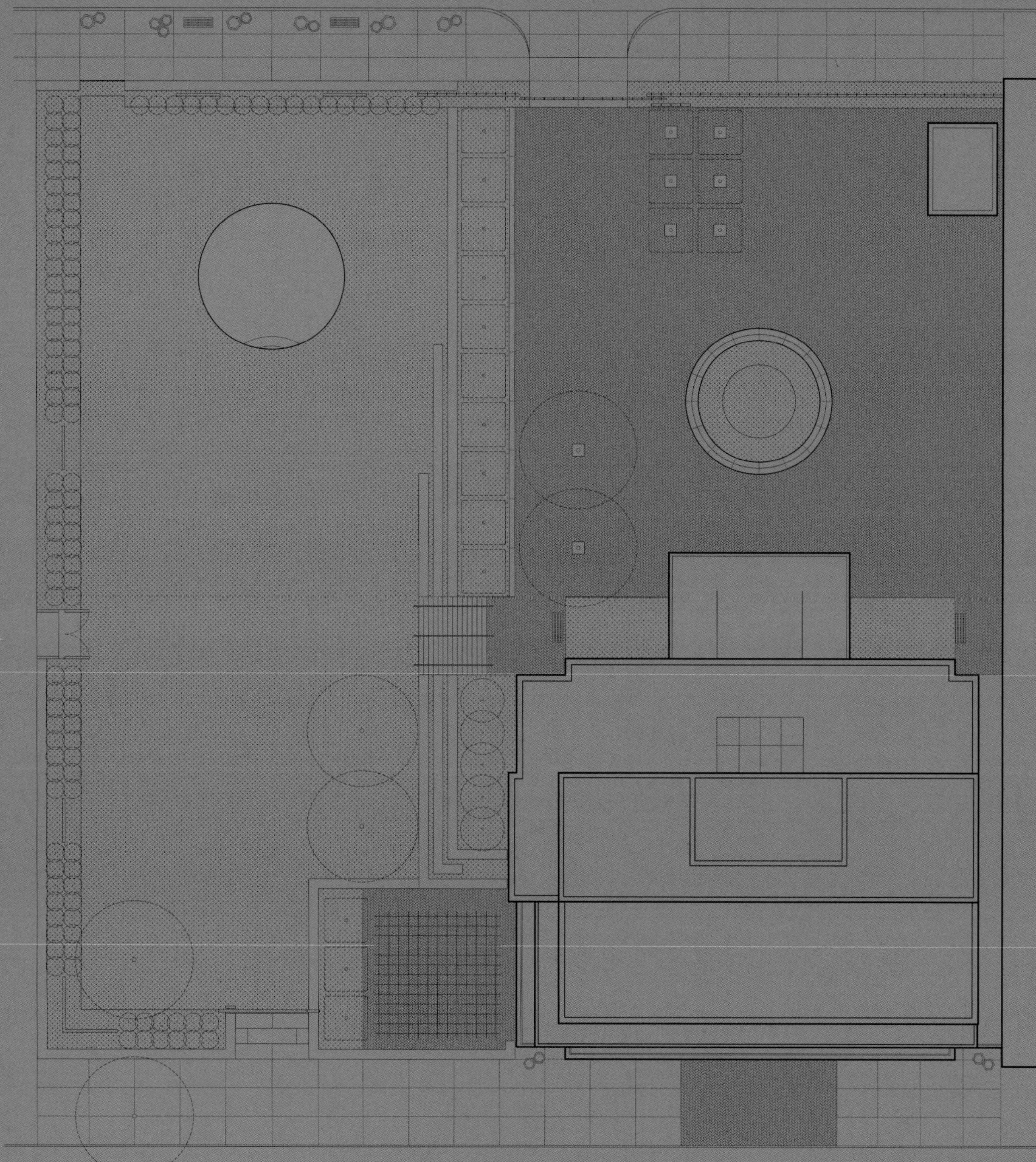

SITE PLAN

LEVEL 1

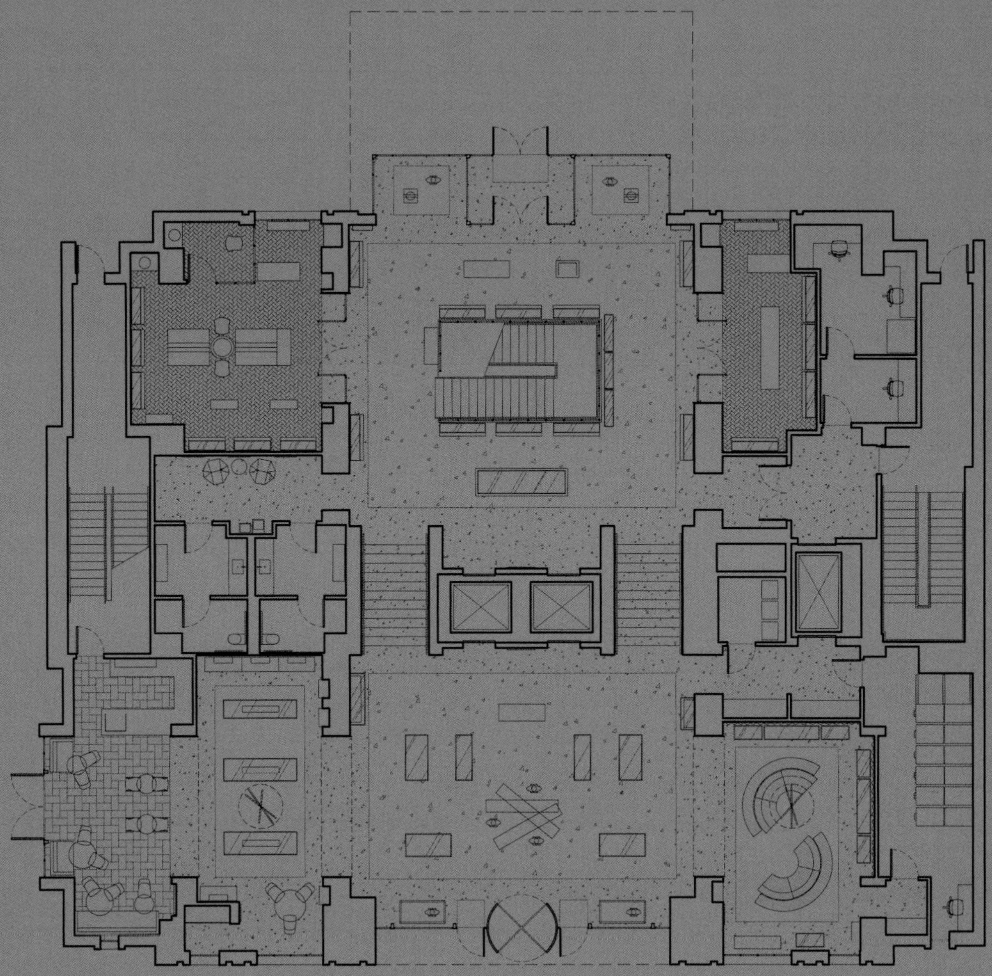

LEVEL 2

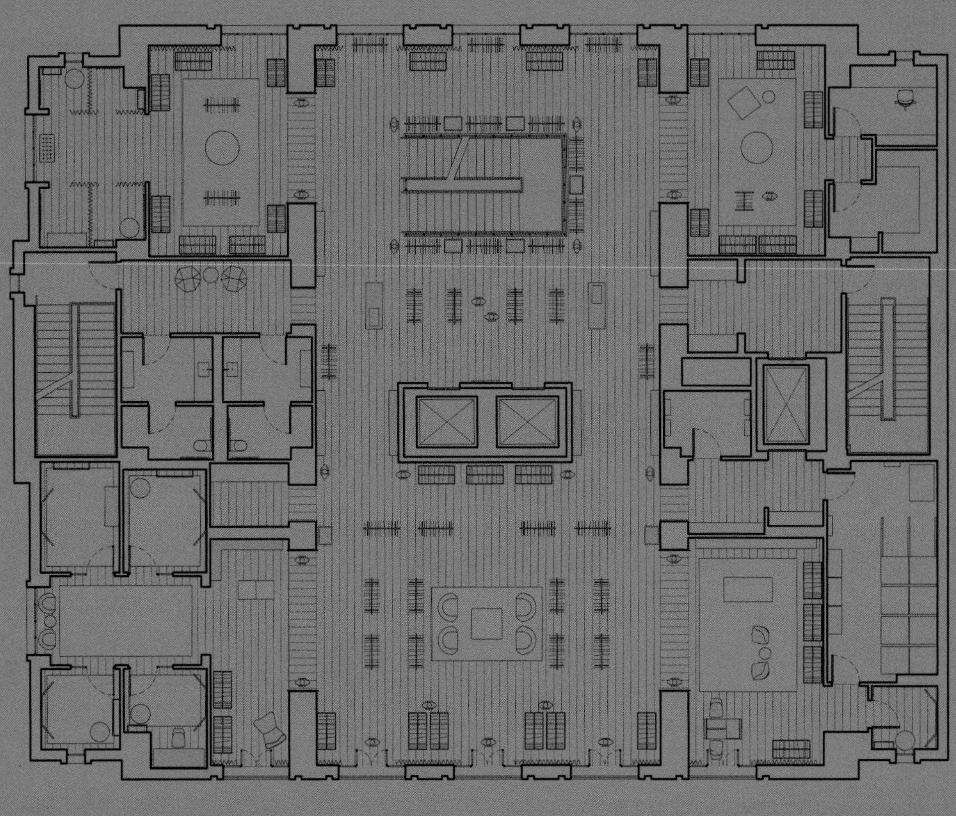

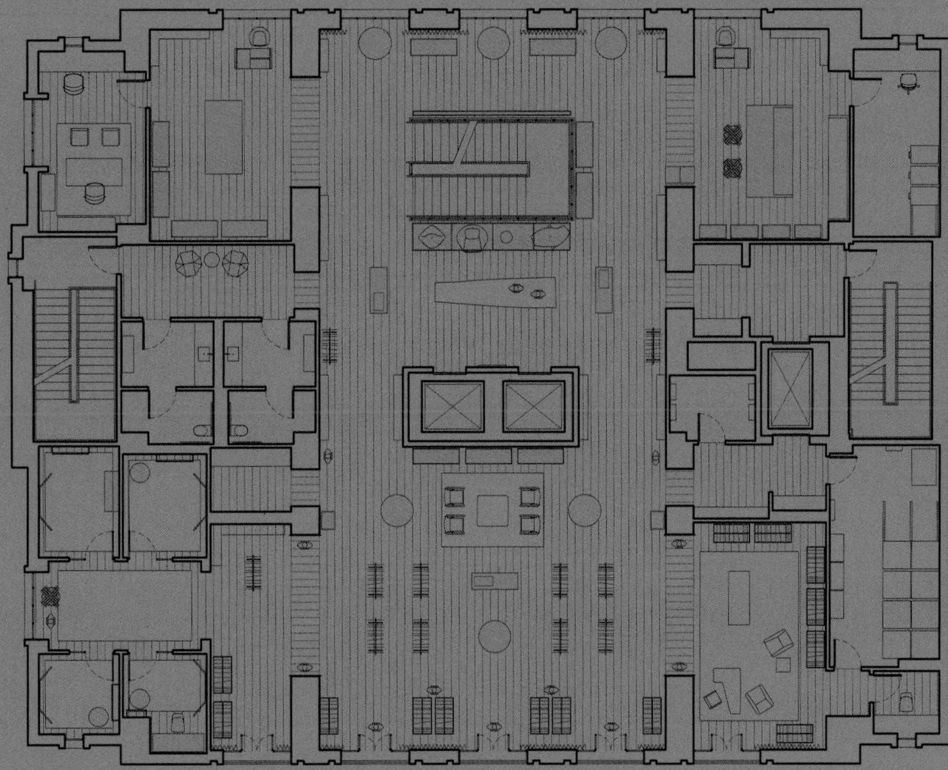

LEVEL 3

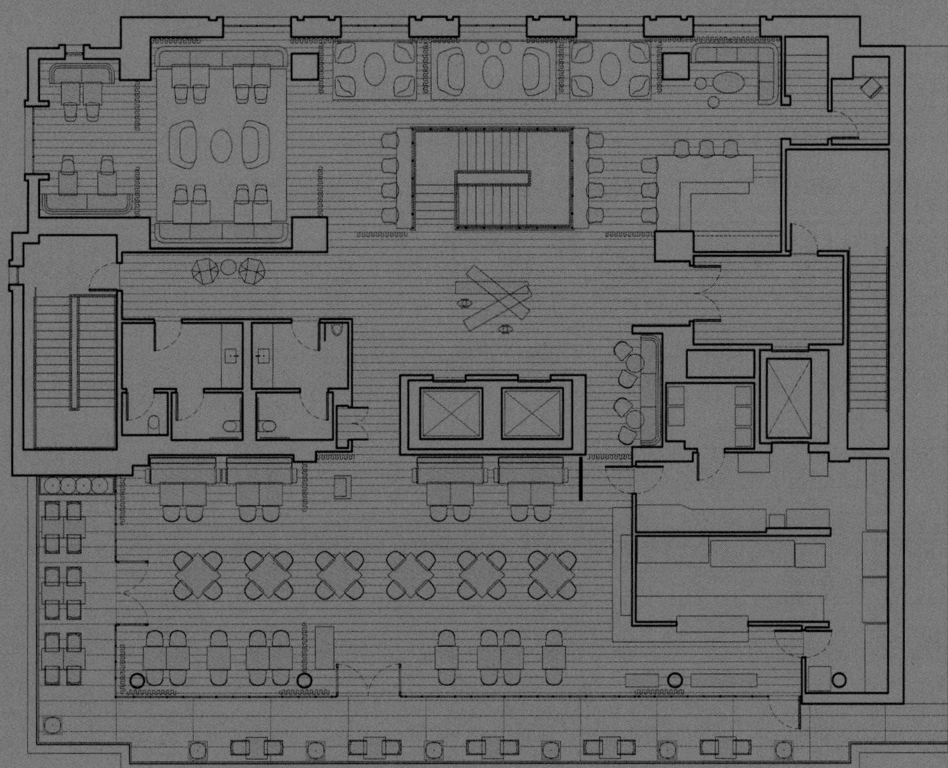

LEVEL 4

The Warehouse

RESERVED
PARKING

14105

FULL
ALEX KATZ
EMMA 2017
NAKAMURA
A Bird in its Existence... 2013
PZ CRATING
AK1362
ALEX KATZ
T-FRAME
OFICH0816

UNIFIED
FINE ARTS SERVICES
US
20066
HT
TARA
WALTERS
David Zwirner

THE WAREHOUSE

Cézanne
de Kooning
JIMMIE DURHAM

GROUP SHOWS
PACIFIC STANDARD TIME
THE PAINTING FACTORY
THE PAINTING OF MODERN LIFE 1960s TO NOW
Painting People
COLIN EISLER
PAINTINGS IN THE HERMITAGE
STEWART TABORI & CHANG
The Panza Collection
THE PAPER SCULPTURE BOOK
THE PAPER SCULPTURE BOOK
THE PAPER SCULPTURE
PARKETT
GROUP SHOWS P
TANGUY CALDER
Target Practice: Painting Under Attack 1949–78
Telling Tales
TEXAS SKY
THIS IS NOT TO BE LOOKED AT
MOCA
THIS WILL HAVE BEEN
THROUGH THE EYES OF TEXAS
THROUGH THE EYES OF TEXAS
THROUGH THE LENS
TIPPET RISE ART CENTER
TOP STORIES
TOP STORIES
TOWARDS A NEW MUSEUM
TOWARDS A NEW MUSEUM
TOWARDS A NEW MUSEUM
TRA
AN ANTHOLOGY OF TRIPLE CANDY
troubled waters
TURN ME ON
TURN ME ON
CHRISTIE'S
CHRISTIE'S
TWENTIETH-CENTURY ART OF LATIN AMERICA
GROUP SHOWS T

GROUP SHOWS H
GROUP SHOWS U – V

GROTJAHN "UNTITLED"
NAKAMURA
"SAD BRAIN"
BLUM & POE
SK 372
28765
YOS-0030
ATO 76
Rach 0140
KOONS
DOG-RED ON SILVER PLATE
YUAN CHIA LI
Packed
MasterPak

FGT Untitled (Natural History)
FRAGILE
G4 middle
UNIFIED
NAKA-M-0005

Tom Friedman
Tom Friedman
ELLSWORTH KELLY
Matisse
PICASSO
ELIZABETH PEYTON

DAVID ALTMEJD
Ida Applebroog
Ida Applebroog
Richard AvedoN
Georg Baselitz
TONY BEVAN
Boetti

FIRE EXTINGUISHER

The Conservatory

THE
CONSERVATORY

ATORY

STYLING NATURE

ATORY
LEWIS MILLER
FOR
URBANSTEMS

ALAÏA AFORE ALAÏA
ALAÏA AFORE ALAÏA
Zaha Hadid Architects
Zaha Hadid Architects

EXIT

DAVID YARROW STORYTELLING
DAVID YARROW STORYTELLING

COLLABORATION

Ten Times Over

BRIAN BOLKE

One of my favorite sayings is "One plus one equals three." That's really what a collaboration should be like, in my view: it should add up to more than the sum of its parts. When I'm working with a good collaborator like Droese Raney, I can give them a series of challenges and inspirations and things I want to do. But I don't know everything—even though I pretend to. The firm has always been able to interpret my ideas, say "Okay," and then come back with something better than I ever would've thought. And that's what a collaborative relationship is supposed to be like. Every project we've worked on together kind of morphs into something totally unexpected.

I've been doing this for a very long time. Twenty-five years. But before that, I studied environmental design—I used to call it "architecture that didn't have to stand up." So I do have a background in store planning and design. When I moved to Dallas, I was creative director of store planning for Neiman Marcus. Then I realized I hated it, and I didn't want to work in an office full of architects and designers. It's a problem, because I was one of the last people in the field to not have to deal with computer stuff; I can only hand-draw and hand-letter and hand-detail. But working with Droese Raney, all I have to do is kind of explain what I have in mind. Then things happen. From the get-go, it was just kind of point-and-shoot, surprisingly fun, and unusually stress-free.

By the time we got started working together, multibrand specialty stores were already something of a dying breed. Forty Five Ten got off the ground in 2000, and it was kind of the last generation of that phenomenon. Conservatory opened in 2019, and I think it's about the only one left to have all the different categories—men's, home, jewelry, apothecary—on that level. I'm really proud of that. When Barneys closed, it left kind of a big void in the market. And there are certainly versions of things that we do, but no one's doing it like this. I guess I felt intuitively that Droese Raney could help us pull that off: I'd seen their Billy Reid store, and we'd done a remodeling project together in the past. Honestly, though, what we set out to do with Forty Five Ten and then the

Go big: *Bold design choices were the order of the day when Bolke and Droese Raney teamed up for Forty Five Ten. On a visit to the Knoll offices in New York, Bolke inspected a prototype display fixture designed by Rem Koolhaas.*

***The art of shopping:** Creativity and bold ideas are everywhere at Forty Five Ten, not just in the design. Rotating selections of fine art, including a display of photographs by Catherine Opie, were part of Bolke's original concept.*

Conservatory was of a very different order of magnitude. With those projects, we had to shoehorn something incredibly complex into a very small footprint.

In the case of Forty Five Ten, I knew we could get customers down there once, but if they just came once and never came back, it would be a failure. So we had to say to ourselves, Okay, how do you make it worthwhile for people to keep coming back? And I think one of the things that Droese Raney understood intuitively was that the store was about both vistas and specifics: things that you leaned up close to see, and things that caught your eye from far away. What we succeeded in doing was making a place where, if you came ten times, you would discover something new ten times over, down to just a tiny swatch of textile. One of the most incredible parts of that store is the art curation—like the time we had the Catherine Opie photo exhibition, about seventy photographs detailing Elizabeth Taylor's house and her jewelry collection. Somebody could come there just to see that, and go through fitting rooms and hallways and different places, and they'd actually learn something while they were shopping. With things like that, maybe they'd only come back once a month. But they would come back.

That shows you the power of creating a total environment, and of designing it the right way. You also had to have a place where there was the built-in ability to change things, to move the furniture around. Maybe my favorite thing at Forty Five Ten was those Rem Koolhaas pieces from Knoll, those plinth-type fixtures. They were incredible—I still don't even know how they worked. But they could just morph and change and become whatever we wanted them to be. Again, I wanted something that, even though it was primarily a fashion store, would be a place for somebody who just loved design to go "What *is* that thing?" Features like the Koolhaas pieces make for a more nuanced project. Even following the opening, after I moved on, we still got these beautiful photos that will live forever, showing what it was really meant to be. When it opened I honestly think it was the most beautiful store in the country, maybe the world.

It's a tough business, doing retail locations. But I love familiarity. I like working with the same people. I always strive to get it right, but I think in this business you never get it *totally* right. You're never going to go, Well, that was a perfect project. I mean maybe when I'm dead, maybe I'll be able to say I got it right, I did everything I wanted to do. But that's why I love retail—the opportunity to reinvent everything, to do something different, paint the whole place pink, do something really wild that you'd never think to do with, say, a house. Anyhow, that's why I came back to Droese Raney to do the Conservatory brand. We really had a kind of a blank slate to create it in 2019, to see our approach evolve a bit. We set out to create something new, that wasn't like Forty Five Ten, and we did. It was such an entirely different situation from our previous project, and it was different with each of the Conservatory locations we've created: at the Hudson Yards branch of Conservatory, the original one, it was almost overcome with people; for the second one, in Highland Park Village, you don't have that natural traffic, you have to draw people in. But in each case, we made it work, and that's what made Conservatory so special.

That just shows you, if you pick the right people and the right touch points from the beginning, you're building on a solid foundation. Droese Raney already had such a strong background being part of a team, working with artisans and so on, and I think we were really able to evolve together in that spirit, to build on that collaborative essence. It's not about ego; it's not about what I want or about what the architects want; it's about the project itself. And I talk about that idea in this business all the time: it's about the company, the brand, which is a living, breathing thing. You have to work with collaborators that are all there for the right reason, and that reason has to be the finished product and making it good, full stop. It's not about your portfolio, it's not about working on a time frame that's the best for the architecture firm. It's not about any of those things. It's simply about what is the best project in the end. And it can be a $5,000 project or a $5 million project or a $50 million project. It really shouldn't matter.

Doubling down: *Bolke asked Droese Raney to take on the Forty Five Ten flagship in downtown Dallas after the firm remodeled the original location on Dallas's McKinney Avenue.*

Picture perfect: *After Forty Five Ten, Bolke asked Droese Raney to develop the retail spaces for his new venture, the Conservatory. Bolke and the firm's Christine Howitt are all smiles at the store in Highland Park Village, Dallas.*

Nick Cave Forothermore
Nick Cave Forothermore
Nick Cave Forothermore

BRICE MARDEN
NICOLEHOLLIS CURATED INTERIORS
NICOLEHOLLIS CURATED INTERIORS
NICOLEHOLLIS CURATED INTERIORS
NICOLEHOLLIS CURATED INTERIORS
SHIGERU BAN TIMBER IN ARCHITECTURE
SHIGERU BAN TIMBER IN ARCHITECTURE
SHIGERU BAN TIMBER IN ARCHITECTURE
SHIGERU BAN TIMBER IN ARCHITECTURE
SHIGERU BAN TIMBER IN ARCHITECTURE

Santa Fe
Modern
JACQUES GRANGE
JACQUES GRANGE
JACQUES GRANGE

DESIGN X CULTURE

Taking their show on the road, the Dallas team builds for art and dialogue, creating an unlikely international connection (and making a few friends) along the way.

Guadalajara is about a thousand miles from Dallas as the crow flies; by plane, the journey takes all of two and a half hours. From the air, the massive city appears suddenly on the floor of the Atemajac Valley, a mat of gray floating on an olive-drab sea. Somewhere down below, down in that vast landscape of ancient cathedrals and sparkling new towers, Droese Raney chanced on a unique source of inspiration, a cultural current that now flows through their entire practice. To understand how, the easiest thing is to actually go to Guadalajara—to walk its crazy streets and stop in for a *trago* at one of its tequilerias, then wander over to the Zona Industrial, past the huge and humming sheds producing exceptional pottery, glass, and metalwork. Barring that, one could just stay in Dallas, go to JOSÉ, and order a skirt steak taco. A white-and-black tile mural along one side of the restaurant tells the story of the project team, their sojourns in Guadalajara, and the improbable dialogue they've helped create between their hometown and Mexico's underappreciated second city.

José was originally a man—still is, in fact: José Noé Suro, a Guadalajara-based tile manufacturer and international art collector the Droese Raney team met while working on their Forty Five Ten project. The instant chemistry between the architects and the proprietor of Ceramica Suro evolved into an enduring friendship that has brought the Dallasites back to the Jalisco capital again and again, deepening their connection to the city, to Suro, and to the scores of young creatives orbiting the Mexican impresario, a remarkable freemasonry of talent that has helped transform a hard-edged factory town into a culturally vibrant hub. To translate some of that artistic sensibility, and some of that lifestyle, to the Dallas food scene, Droese Raney teamed up with local restaurateurs Brady and Megan Wood to bring José—the restaurant—to a formerly tired stretch at the western end of Lover's Lane in Bluffview.

The establishment occupies a modest two-story envelope with a half-concealed pitched roof, the latter a concession to local building codes, which also imposed conditions for parking and building use on the cramped suburban site. Technically a refurbishment of a former dry cleaner, the design preserves most of the original steel frame but masks it with a distinctly Mexican brick facade with squared and cruciform apertures that allow glimpses from the street into the welcoming interior. Once inside, guests find generous banquettes lined in bright-yellow upholstery, a glittering bar with (naturally) an impressive tequila collection, and an inventive indoor-outdoor disposition. A retractable roof allows a portion of the dining room to be opened to the elements, instantly transforming it into a breezy patio exactly like those that fill the backways of Guadalajara. Driving the narrative home is the monumental tilework covering the wall above some booths: in bold, sketch-style strokes, the piece presents a series of Guadalajaran street-life vignettes, including images of the restaurant's namesake, its founders, and its designers.

One outgrowth of that group's free-spirited artistic and culinary collaboration happens to be sitting right next door. One of the international band of dreamers and makers behind José is a Dallas business magnate who first joined the team almost by way of happenstance: he owns the property where José now stands. Becoming more and more involved with the restaurant's development and enraptured by the lively, sociable ambience he found there, the businessman ultimately stepped away from his work in the corporate world and decided to open up a PERSONAL OFFICE in the building immediately adjacent to José, evolving from landlord into dedicated patron and chief in-house bon vivant.

Reflecting that position, the office he commissioned from Droese Raney is as much about pleasure as about business, a minipalace for relaxed deal making. Like José, the design entailed bureaucratic hoop-jumping, requiring the sharing with its neighbor of on-site car spaces and the adoption of a similarly peaked roofline. Other than this component, however, the office is remarkably different: where the restaurant shields its diners (and its gable) behind its brick screen, the office opens up proudly to the street, presenting itself as a sort of asymmetrical chalet with a prominent second story. The latter, which sits atop a work suite, is the highlight of the private office, an impressive space that opens up immediately to a large terrace featuring impressive plantings, technically daring water features, and bespoke seating, all co-created with landscape architect Hocker. Sleek, contemporary, with plenty of room to stretch out, the office represents a slightly (but only slightly) more formal take on the restaurant's easy subtropical nature: Guadalajara on a Dallas work trip.

Mexico—or rather the celebrated intersection of the Mexican and Texan identities—provides the theme for another Droese Raney restaurant interior, MI COCINA in Klyde Warren Park, which serves elegant atmospherics alongside phenomenal Tex-Mex fare. The downtown outpost is only one of the Dallas mainstay's two dozen branches, with others (in particular the one in posh Highland Park Village, also created by the firm) demonstrating a similarly sophisticated vibe. Even so, the Klyde Warren restaurant stands out, as much for its high-profile site as for the assorted architectural and historical threads its designers weave together.

Capping what was previously the open trench of the Woodall Rogers Freeway, Klyde Warren Park has turned a once-barren stretch of the center city into an area buzzing with life, providing a shared front lawn for the nearby Nasher Sculpture Center, Dallas Museum of Art, and Myerson Symphony Center, among other institutions in the Arts District. Mi Cocina occupies the park's primary physical armature: a graceful public pavilion, clad in transparent glass and topped by a razor-thin roof, from architect Thomas Phifer. Droese Raney's interior solution preserves the integrity of the Phifer design; at the same time, it introduces a quantum of volcanic, Mesoamerican flair, courtesy of a sculptural central service core hewn from rough lava rock, dramatically lit from above, and hung with colorful portraits and floral paintings. Together with custom furniture and a muscular, textural material palette of wood, metal, and natural fabric, the design brings the artisanal traditions of the architects' beloved Mexico into the very heart of Dallas, connecting the city's new cultural acropolis to the world beyond—and adding another chapter to Droese Raney's ongoing tale of cross-border exchange.

José

Topo Chico

JOSÉ

LA

ASAMIGOS

SALADITAS

Topo Chico
JOSE

PUSH

TVELOVEJTLOLTVLE

JOSÉ

Personal Office

Mi Cocina

ENTRY

LA PARADA
Order Here
DOUBLE DOUBLE BURGER 12.45
BRISKET AVOCADO MELT 12.45
GRILLED CHEESE 6.95
TINGA QUESADILLA 6.95
BRISKET TAQUITOS 9.95
NACHOS AZTECAS 11.45
CRISPY BEEF TACOS 7.85
SMOKY SHRIMP COCKTAIL 12.45
QUESO FRIES 6.85
SIDES
CRISPY FRIES 3 95
GUACAMOLE 6 95
SALSA 3 95
TEXAS TRES WAY 8 95
BEVS
WATER 4.00
COKE
DIET COKE
SPRITE
DR PEPPER
MICHELOB ULTRA

LA PARADA
Pick Up
Baños

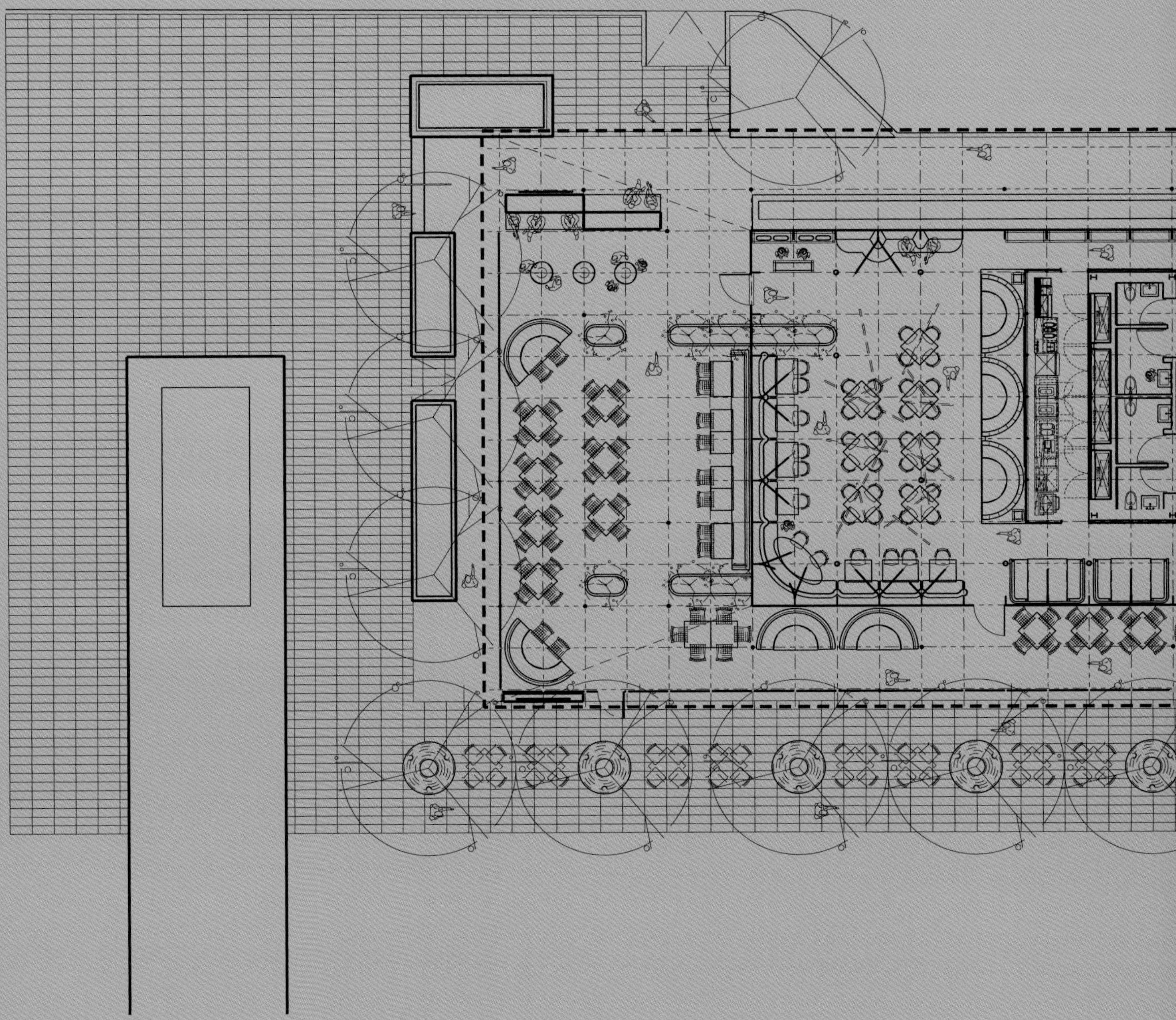

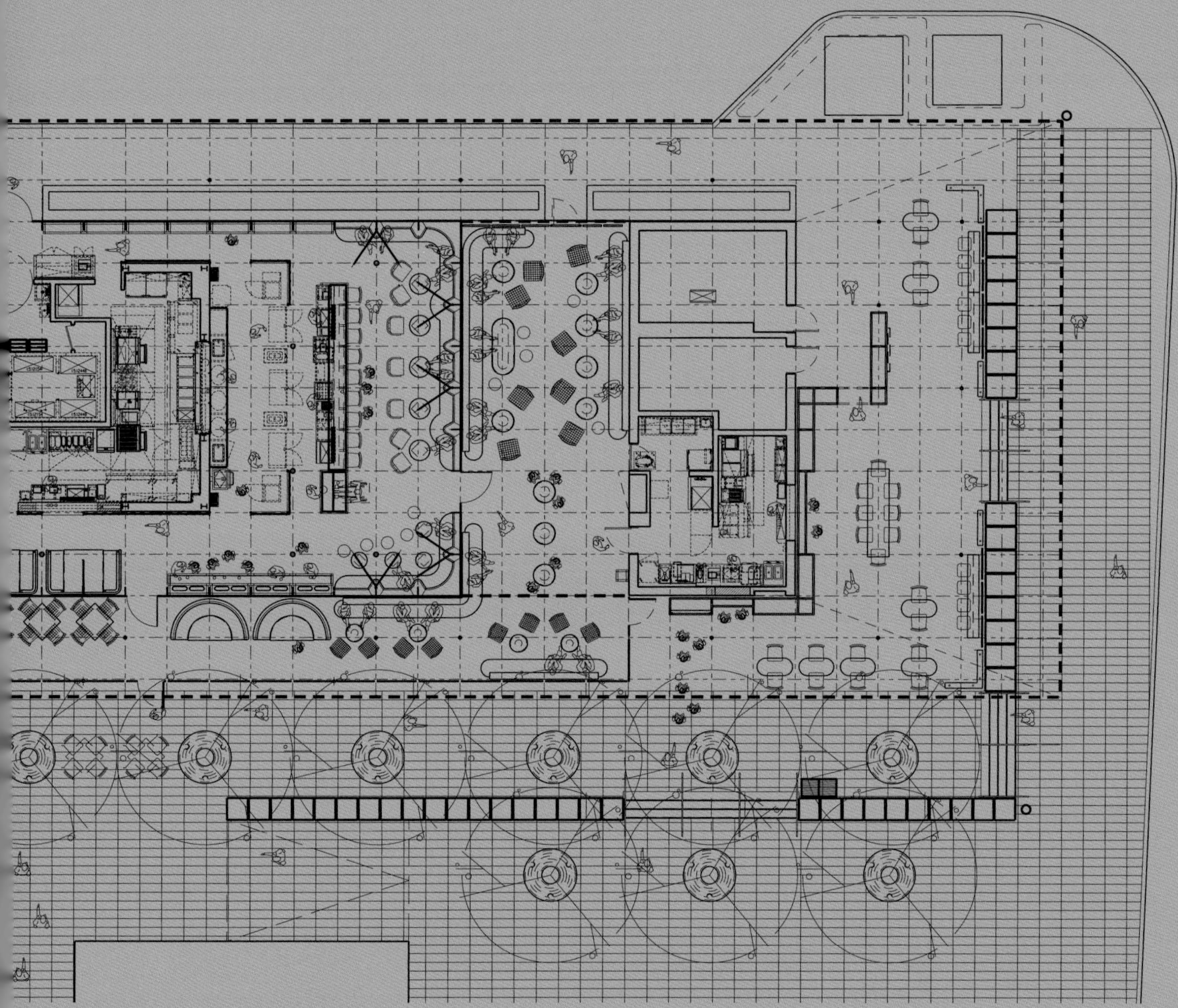

Frozen / Skinny

siembra valle
reposado
EL TESORO
EXTRA AÑEJO
TEQUILA
FUENTESECA
RESERVA
1146
1942
ARETTE
BOZAL
BANHEZ
ESPADIN & BARRIL
CASAMIGOS
MEZCAL
DIPLOMÁTICO
HERRADURA
AÑEJO

DESIGN X BALANCE

Four projects; four (very different) clients; four feats of architectural derring-do: witness the spectacular high-wire act of Droese Raney.

What do the downtown apartment of a notorious society doyenne, a rustic ranch on the Brazos River, a breakthrough 90s-cool suburban villa, and a meticulous reconstruction of a lost midcentury masterpiece have in common? Not much—except that each of them required a certain kind of design practice, one capable of straddling unusual contradictions and holding together opposing ideas. For Droese Raney, the unusual scope of their competency pairs with a related quality, one that is evident in so many of their disparate projects: a willingness to go out on a precarious-seeming limb in the service of a concept or a client, and then somehow return, seemingly unscathed, to earth.

This unusual mix of daring and equilibrium proved an essential asset in the creation of ANGIE'S CONDO. One of Dallas's most glamorous public figures, celebrated for her outsized public presence and keen fashion sense, the titular resident would ordinarily be expected to occupy a sprawling pile in Highland Park—as indeed she had before embarking on a new phase of her life with the purchase of a pair of adjacent units at One Arts Plaza in the Arts District. The move itself was typical of the client's enterprising spirit: the building had yet to be completed; the neighborhood was not, at the time, the hotspot it has since become; and the entire idea of a Dallas woman of culture and means living in a high-rise apartment appeared, to most locals, rather eccentric. A New Yorker could live in a loft. But a Dallasite?

The architects answered that question with an interior that strikes an edifying balance between the competing imperatives of the brief. Beginning with an inventive floor plan that combined the two apartments into one, the team set about adding custom details and fixtures, including a sleek kitchen from German supplier Bulthaup and bespoke window and floor treatments from local artist Julie Cohn, all while remaining within the building's mandatory design guidelines. Making room for its owner's extensive art collection (including works by Dan Flavin, Andreas Gursky, and others), the minimalist set of rooms exudes just enough glam to compliment some of her more unusual possessions (an electric massage bed, for example), while its wide-open central living room makes the most of its ample footprint, the sense of space enough to impress even the mansion set. A definitive statement on the possibilities of urban living in Dallas, the project blazed a trail for thousands more high-end condos in the area.

Halfway across Texas is the small town of Goree. A world apart from the cushy confines of the big city, the old-fashioned frontier community comprises little more than a post office and a few houses. Yet immediately outside of town, Droese Raney imported a sophistication rarely seen in these parts. On a property that had been in the client's family since the mid-nineteenth century, the designers turned a modest proposal for a rural getaway into the **FLYING R RANCH**, a welcoming setting for festive get-togethers that lure family and friends from all over.

Dividing the plan into discrete units, the architects created separate living quarters for the client's children and grandchildren, simultaneously expanding both the functional value and the planar intricacy of the scheme. All of the volumes are oriented for maximal views of the river and surrounding plains in an arrangement that slowly reveals itself. As visitors arrive from the road and proceed up a long, curving path toward the compound, low profiles conceal the structures' true size as well as the expansive landscape beyond. On closer inspection, the spartan envelopes are revealed to be elegant, commodious compositions of steel and stone, as sharp and contemporary as their environs are rough and timeless. They project the same glassy calm as the lazy Brazos, which is visible from nearly every window.

Back in Dallas proper, the **RHEIMS RESIDENCE** represents yet another turning point for the firm and for their hometown—one that might easily have gone a different way but for Droese Raney's careful, calibrated approach. Among the office's earliest ground-up projects, the pre-2000 commission shows the designers' unique sensibility already in place, along with their deft hand for managing a potentially fraught context: the clients, a young couple who had never worked with an architect before; the immediate vicinity, a street full of large but stylistically staid single-family houses in a demure Dallas neighborhood; and, just to add one more wrinkle, the lot, which contained one of the oldest trees in the city, a non-negotiable fixture of any site plan the architects might devise.

Though mindful of the leafy landmark, little else about Droese Raney's solution could be called conservative, at least not in concept. In place of the historicism favored by the Tudor, French Renaissance, and Mission-style neighbors, the architects opted for a recognizable yet very specific modernist language, a sort of meditation on 1900s-era Prairie school design but with a stripped-down, Y2K twist. Featuring some of the only custom wooden windows anywhere in Dallas, the design pairs Wrightian organicism with an urbane atmosphere conjured through Lueders white Texas limestone blocks and graceful metal details; its airy, sunlit interior opens onto a remarkably formal landscape. The combination of ease and orderliness seems perfectly tailored to a couple just settling into domestic life, and to a community (and a city) still growing accustomed to forward-thinking residential architecture.

As much as Droese Raney has helped push Dallas architecture forward, one of its most audacious performances to date has involved going back in time. From the 1920s clear through to the 1970s, the name of Charles Dilbeck was all but synonymous with northeastern Texas: the Tulsa native designed some 300 residential projects in the region, from fanciful Swiss chalets and Disneyish minicastles to low-slung, "good life" modernist ranch houses. One of his most striking later works in the latter mode is the **GEISLER RESIDENCE** (originally the Lobello House), built in 1962 and featuring Dilbeck's signature recipe of structural finesse, hyper-refined craftsmanship, and processional complexity. Behind a deceptively conventional exterior of stone cladding and pitched roofs, visitors discover a dense, clusterlike plan of interconnecting spaces fairly teeming with spatial modulations and exquisite detailing. Or that's what visitors *used* to discover there—until the house burned down, only a very short while after its current owners bought it.

Their solution: get Droese Raney to build the house back exactly as it was, beginning with nothing save a portion of the grand fireplace that survived the blaze. Wading through Dilbeck's archives at the University of Texas, the architects found some of the master's original drawings for the project and used them to reconstruct his design process. Everything—from the theatrical brass doorknobs to the unlikely intersections of the gables to the dentil trim around the entrance marquee, which required specially built knives to cut to just the right specifications—was replicated precisely as it had been fifty years earlier, bringing the house and all of its lost splendor back to life. If previous projects had seen Droese Raney walk some very narrow tightropes, this one required them to do so while bearing a very large architectural legacy over their shoulders. With almost outrageous courage, they accepted the challenge, then met it with astonishing restraint.

Angie's Condo

Alberto Giacometti
Paul Klee
MARC CHAGALL
DADA & SURREALIST ART
CHAIM GROSS
LARRY RIVERS
JULES OLITSKI
ELLSWORTH KELLY
MAX WEBER
JASPER JOHNS
Sam Francis
ROBERT MOTHERWELL
Yves Klein
CHRISTO
LUCAS SAMARAS
MORRIS LOUIS
RAUSCHENBERG
ROY LICHTENSTEIN
ROTHKO
CHUCK CLOSE
JULIUS SHULMAN
MODERNISM
MAPPLETHORPE
BY ANDY WARHOL
WARHOL
ANDY WARHOL
EDWARD RUSCHA
KANDINSKY
THE NASHER COLLECTION
DAVID HOCKNEY BY
KANDINSKY
THE HAMPTONS
AMERICAN FASHION

Flying R Ranch

West

TEXAS MODERN

Rheims Residence

Geisler Residence

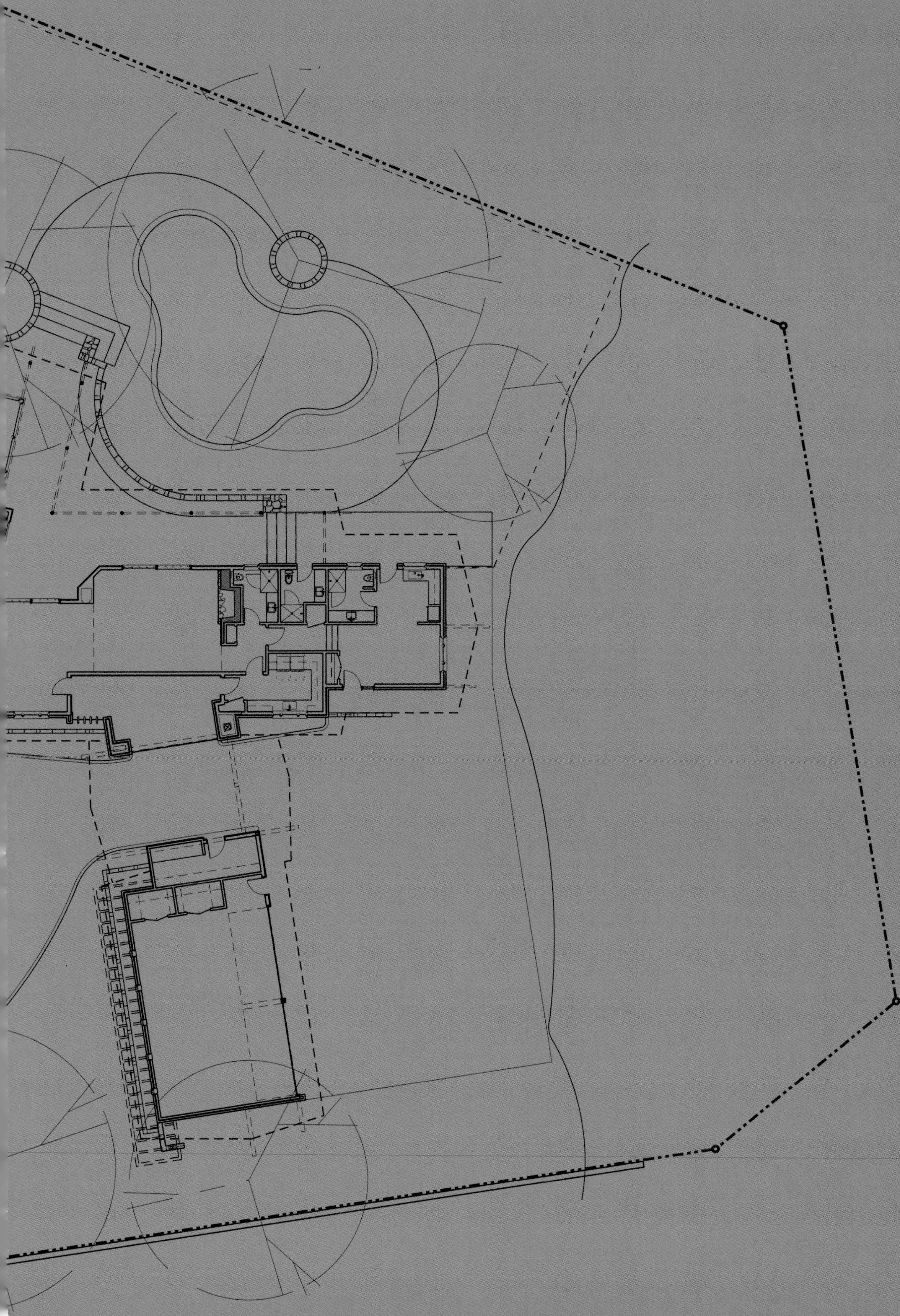

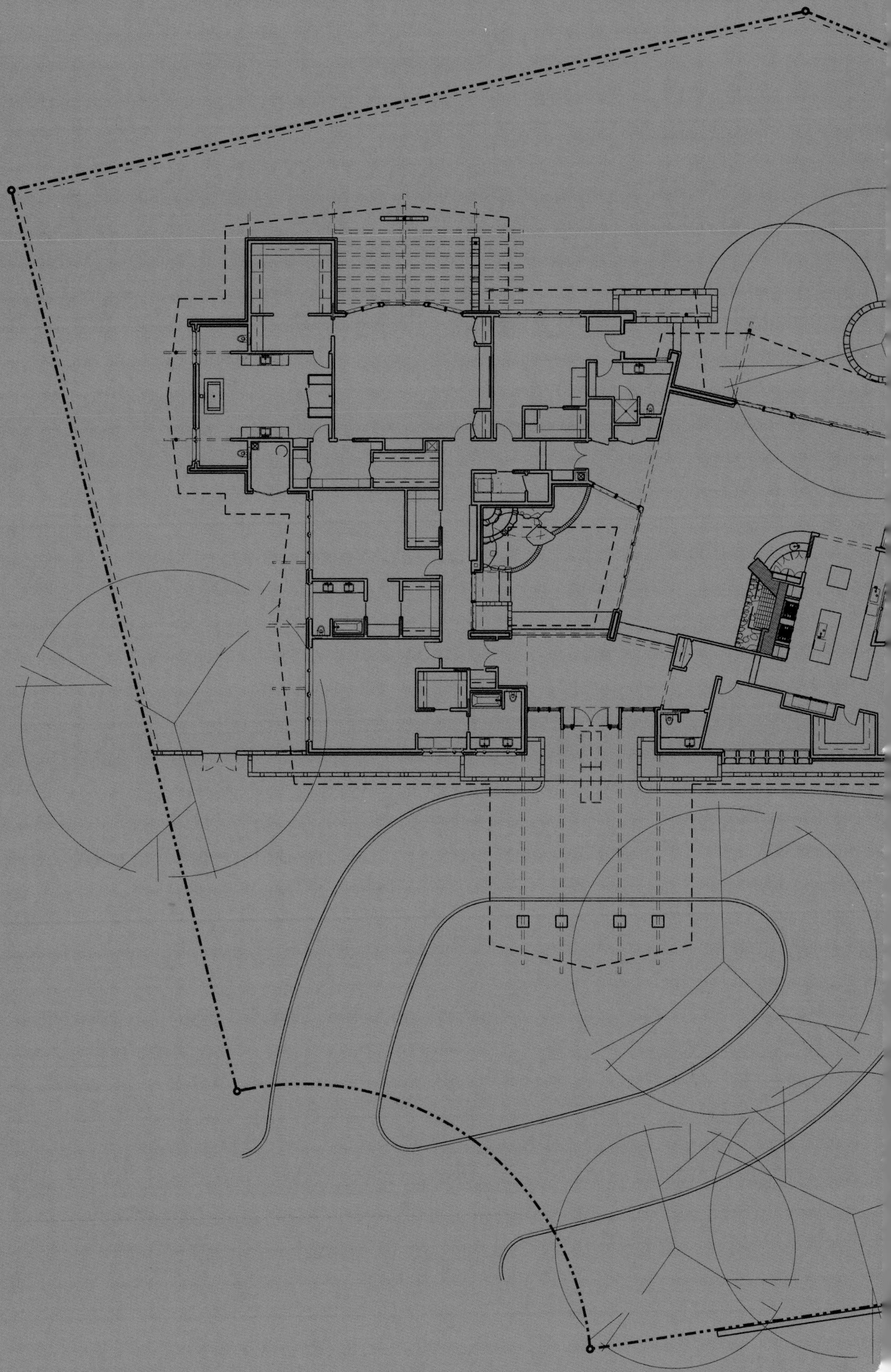

joy

DESIGN X VISION

After twenty-five years and dozens of projects, it's still about friends, family, and creating something new.

It didn't seem like a great place to put an architecture studio. In 2012, the corner of Sylvan Avenue and Pollard Street was on the wrong side of everything—of the tracks, the river, the freeway. Even by the standards of the neighborhood, there was something less than seemly about the parcel; surrounded by a dusty margin of grass and gravel, the brick-and-cinderblock warehouse and low-rise outbuildings looked like nothing so much as pure, all-American junkspace, a backdrop for the often unsavory business of the block.

Establishing the SYLVAN/POLLARD office did not come easy to Droese Raney. Besides the lingering presence of the local criminal element, the technical challenges in converting the single-story structure into a spacious, comfortable workplace proved remarkably steep: skylights had to be cut into the roof, an entirely new mechanical system had to be installed, and at one point the building itself started to give way, the masonry falling off the facade and into the street. While staving off total collapse, the designers also managed to transform the envelope almost beyond recognition, turning a small corner window into a glazed storefront and exchanging a series of awkward gutter pipes for projecting spouts near the flat roofline. A couple coats of gray-beige paint, a sprinkling of prickly pears, one perforated-steel sliding door—and presto! The corner was born again, an oasis of hip in the dusty quasi-urban desert.

Today, the rough edges of the neighborhood are largely gone, replaced by multifamily developments and commercial storefronts. The architects' arrival doubtless helped to catalyze this change—but for all that the rehabilitated building has meant to the area, the experience of working there, of inhabiting the environment that they created, has meant no less to the firm. Light and open, simple and spare, the space is as succinct a declaration of the designers' architectural values as one is likely to find anywhere in their portfolio, and its intimacy of scale (more pronounced even than in many smaller studios) avoids the factory-floor effect so common in the profession. The interior is a sort of concentrated expression of Droese Raney's ethos and history: the crates that form a perimeter around the conference room, donated to the practice by client and collector Howard Rachofsky and the Dallas Museum of Art, formerly housed a large piece by artist Julian Schnabel; the wood that forms the partners' large shared worktable was salvaged from a Fort Worth brewery and polished with a floor sander by the partners themselves. In the rear, display shelves hold items gathered along the team's assorted journeys and creative encounters: old iPhones and statues of the Empire State Building, rocks with holes and lenses from an old film projector.

What it all speaks to, and what sustained the project from its not altogether promising beginning, is a particular kind of far-seeing faith: a faith in people, and in the connections between them, to produce great things. The most impressive testament to that conviction is housed in the smaller warehouse structure next door, formerly belonging to an auto-body chop shop and now affording a place for meetings with friends and collaborators and coworkers as well as a repository of some of the architects' larger memorabilia. Openable to the out-of-doors, the social distancing–friendly space launched during the pandemic with an art exhibition and soon became a favorite redoubt of the broader Droese Raney community. It has slowly accumulated a veritable treasure trove of material samples, architecture books, and as astounding a selection of rare tequilas and mezcals as is to be found anywhere this side of the Sierra Madre Occidental—many in outrageously sculptural bottles, boots and guitars and skeletal señoritas. Droese and Raney's motorcycle collection is in there too, and after hours the team will retreat to the shed for a lengthy hang sesh. Leaning up against a Ducati, or perched on one of the barstools designed by the firm, one architect will talk about an upcoming project or a past one while another architect will tell the story of a recent trip to Guadalajara or start dreaming up the next visit to New York. Eventually they'll filter out, back into the Dallas night, through the streets of the city they've spent over two decades helping to build. They might go far, but they'll never be out of reach, and they'll always know how to find their way back.

Sylvan/Pollard

DROESE RANEY
ARCHITECTURE

HOUSES of MEXICO
PATIOS AND GARDENS OF MEXICO
HOUSES of MEXICO
MEXICAN INTERIORS
THE ARCHITECTURE OF TREES

← FLIGHT DIRECTION →
FRAGILE
FRAGILE
artemis

ROJAS CONSTR.
R L UPHOLSTERY

EXIT

ARCHITECTURE NOW!
New York 1960
AMALFI

RACH
0008 B
FRAGILE

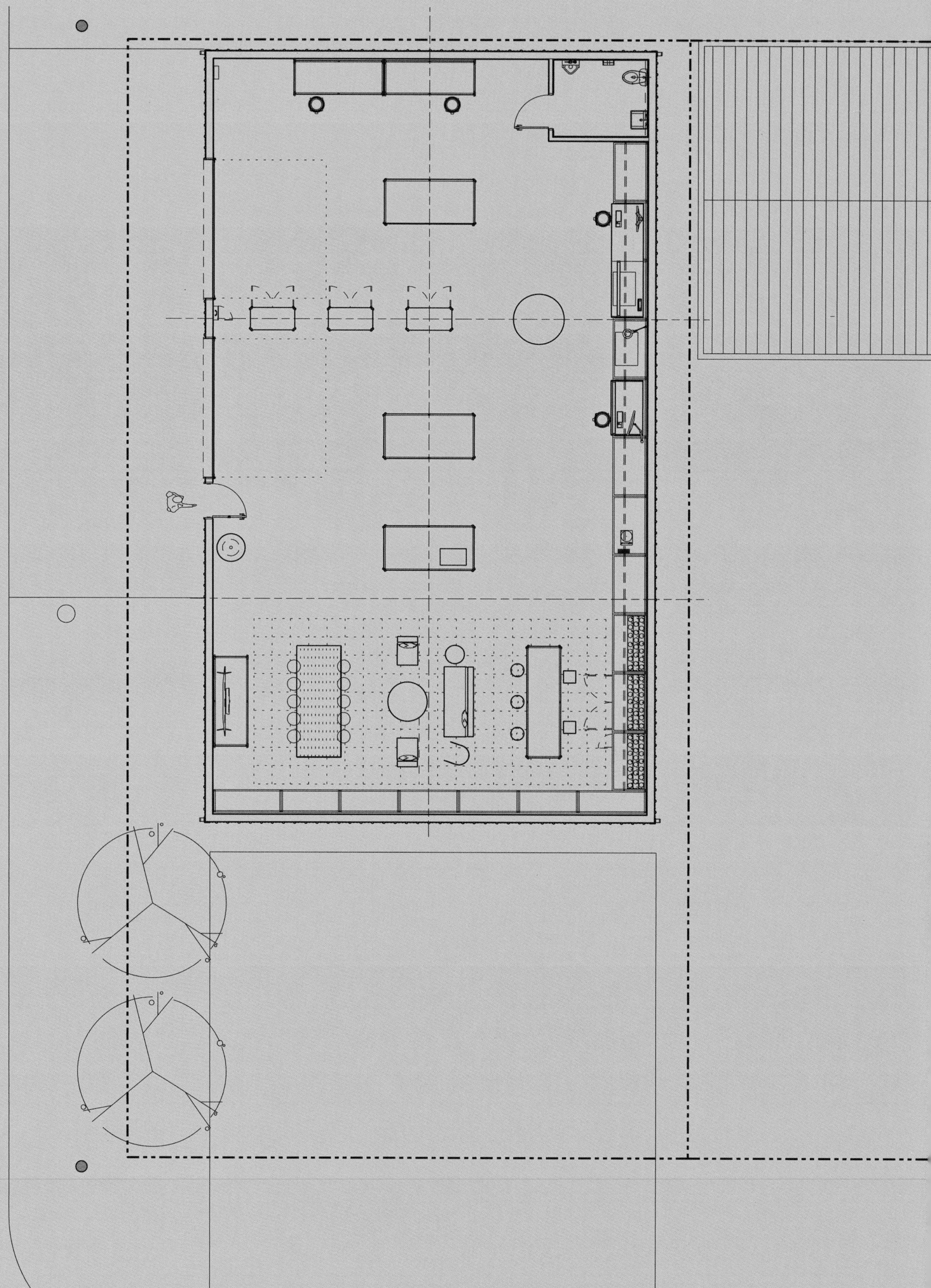

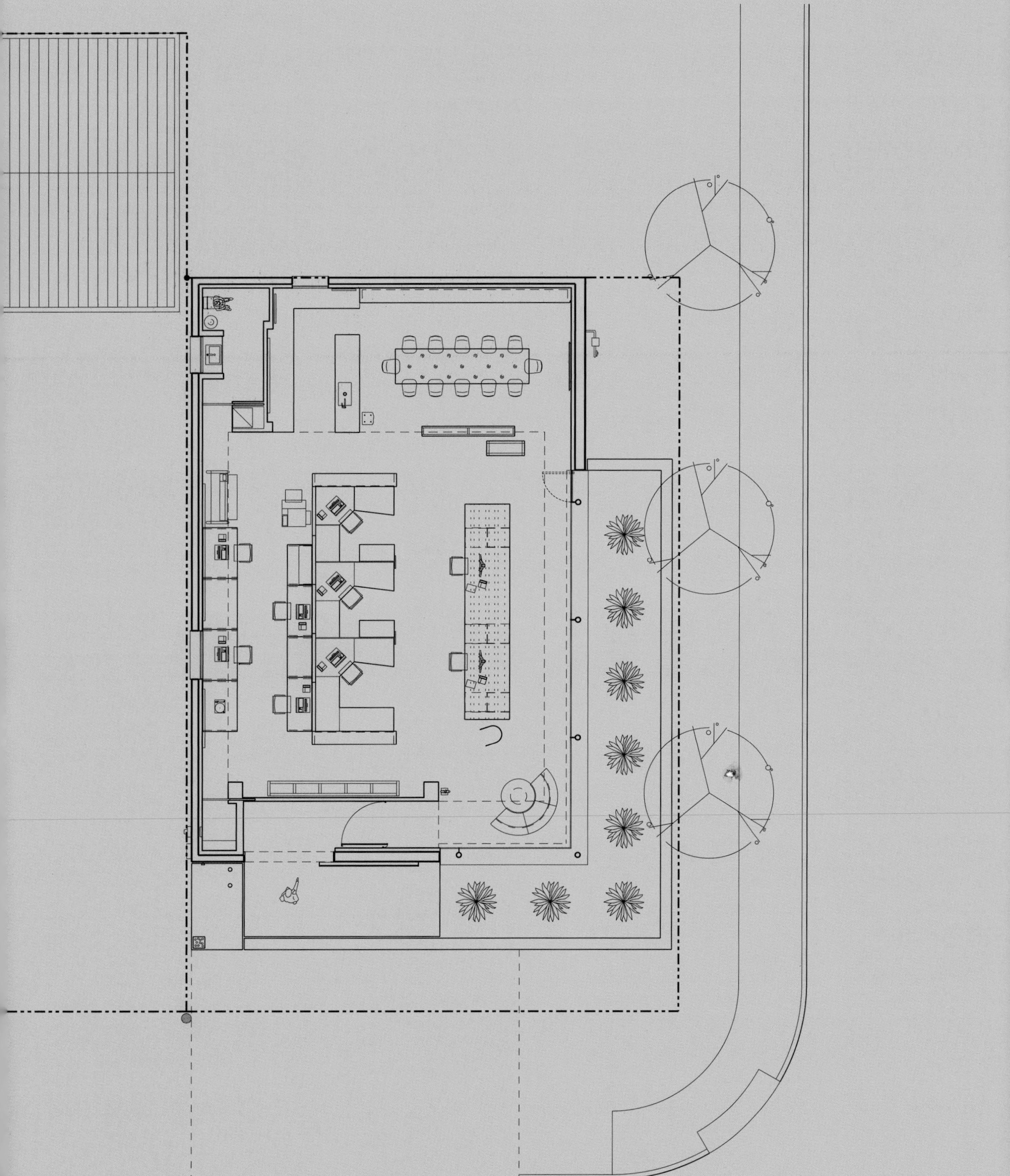

COLLABORATION

This Is the Way

DAVID DROESE, LANCE RANEY,
CHRISTINE HOWITT, REID MULLIGAN

David: I never doubted we would get to this point in our career. But the odds were not exactly in our favor. The vast majority of designers, young ones, who set up practices of their own—they're usually one of two kinds of people: the kind who work for years at a big national or international practice, who have clients they can bring with them; or the kind who have a lot of their own money to start out with, family money. Or they're both. We weren't either of those things. We did it basically for fun—for our love of design and drawing, in the beginning. Which sounds a little insane in retrospect, but I guess we had a feeling about it.

Lance: It was the two of us in a room with a door, two sawhorses, and a couple laptops. When we'd travel together, not that that was often, we would usually stay in the same hotel room. We had this dream of what we wanted, but it wasn't superstardom or to strike it rich or anything like that. What we really dreamed about was being able to buy a couple of Eames chairs. That, to us, was the goal—to get a couple of real, good-looking Eames chairs. And then when we finally did find a pair, it was at a junk sale, and we had to go and totally reupholster them ourselves. Our wives were not happy.

David: It's not like anything changed at any one point after that. We didn't wake up one morning and go, Gee, we're getting a lot of work, look at all these great clients and these big projects we're doing. There were milestones, of course, and we had some idea when we were hitting them: the Rheims House, which was different from most residential projects in the city at the time and got a lot of coverage; Forty Five Ten, obviously, which showed what we could do on a larger scale and in a complicated urban situation; the Warehouse, anyone would give their left arm (only because I draw with my right) to work with Howard; the Billy Reid store in Manhattan, which, just because of where it is, you knew, okay, *something* different is happening with this practice. But it all happened one after the other. It wasn't premeditated, and we didn't see any of it coming. We never really paused to think about it.

Some things never change: *Droese and Raney have always been fascinated by the tools of their trade. Material samples and drawing implements are at once essential instruments and studio decor, reminders of projects past and inspiration for projects future.*

The firm that plays together stays together:
The architects rarely turn down a chance to hit the road with friends and collaborators.

Lance: Not till we were doing this book. The truth of the matter is that what we do as architects isn't separate from the other things we do and enjoy and see and believe in: there isn't work-us and not-work-us; there are relationships that become projects, and projects that turn into relationships; everything is sort of on the same plane. When you think about the other voices in this book, you see that happening over and over again. We started out doing an art space for Howard Rachofsky, basically sight unseen, and soon we're talking about art and artists, we're helping renovate his house. With José Noé Suro, it began with trying to find some good tiles, and before you know it, we're spending weeks together in Guadalajara, planning exhibitions in Dallas. When you're in the flow of life like that, it just comes natural.

Christine: Not to make it sound like there wasn't a lot of hard work that goes into all this, but when you think about it, we could get plenty of work done just sitting at our computers; we could do Zoom calls with clients and get the basic info from them, then go out and do some pretty good projects. But that's not what we do. Instead, we go to where the clients are—we go to Alabama, or we go out to Goree, Texas, or wherever—and we spend the time making those connections. Every trip we take together, whether to New York City or to Mexico or just down the block in Dallas, is an experience that draws us closer together. And sure, that makes the projects better in the ordinary sense, helps the store sell more clothes or the bar sell more drinks. But it also makes the work more meaningful, puts each project in a bigger cultural and social frame. You can think of it in the way some writers, some novelists, create their own fictional worlds, with characters that show up in different stories so the reader gets to see them from different angles. There's almost a Droese Raney universe out there, all these people and places that are woven together by our work.

Reid: Which, obviously, is not something that a lot of firms can say. The funny thing is, for Christine and me, this is the only job we've ever had: we literally cannot imagine doing architecture any other way. But you look around and you see how a lot of offices operate, even some amazingly good ones—it's a project here, and a project there, and the only thing that connects them is maybe this one aesthetic quality or this big conceptual idea that the firm's founders have. What we've learned, working with this kind of practice, is that it isn't about the designer's ego; it's about being in the room with the contractor, the fabricator, the developer, the restaurateur, and building the design from that group dynamic. That's where design ideas come from, very often, whether it's how to connect two buildings with a third one, or how to rebuild a fifty-year-old house.

Lance: Staying adaptable, focusing on the here and now, that's the only way we know how to work, and everyone who comes into the office, a new associate or a new client, learns that pretty quick.

David: Whatever happens in the future, it's just going to be about building on the relationships we already have, and building more of them. For us, getting bigger just means including more people. That's what it's all about.

The stuff of memory: *Droese Raney's R&D lab—a former warehouse next to the main studio—displays the designers' collections of art, motorcycles, tequila, and more, producing a visual scrapbook of their shared professional and personal journey.*

Droese Raney X Droese Raney: *The office never sleeps. At night, perforated-steel portraits of Raney and Droese gaze out at the street.*

RANEY
ELGIN
10¢ RENU-BAK
REFRESH YOUR BRASSIERE
ELASTIC · ADJUSTABLE
LIBERTY
WE TRUST
THE LONE BUT NOT LONELY STAR STATE
TEXAS
Neiman Marcus

Smoke
Natural Gray
Sidewalk Gray
Sidewalk Gray
CHARCOAL
CHARLEY BROWN

BENDHEIM
Fade® Glass
BENDHEIM

REID MULLIGAN, LANCE RANEY, DAVID DROESE, CHRISTINE HOWITT, COURTNEY TERRELL

HEATHER MAGEE, JONATHAN MANN, DANIELLE ANDERSON, ROSANA AVINA, MATTHEW GILLEY

PROJECT CREDITS

BILLY REID

New York, New York; Austin, Texas
Client: Billy Reid
Droese Raney: David Droese, Christine Howitt
Photography: Fredrik Brodén, Unknown

NEIGHBORHOOD GOODS

Plano, Texas; New York, New York; Austin, Texas
Client: Mark Masinter and Matt Alexander
Droese Raney: Lance Raney, Ezra Loh, Madison Dahl
Structural Engineer: Ronald A. Roberts Associates, Inc. (Plano)
MEP Engineer: Purdy-McGuire, Inc. (Plano), AMA Consulting Engineers (NY), Wylie Consulting Engineers (Austin)
Lighting Designer: Essential Light Design Studio
Food Service Consultant: Complete Restaurant Services
General Contractor: Scott + Reid General Contractors Inc. (Plano), Wesbuilt (NY), The Burt Group (Austin)
Photography: Fredrik Brodén
Artists/Artisans: Impressions Architectural Millwork, Sarche Concrete Design, Springer Design Studio, Kyle Steed, Huy Nguyen

HATCHWAYS

Dallas, Texas
Client: Rebees
Droese Raney: Lance Raney, Madison Dahl
Structural Engineer: Ronald A. Roberts Associates, Inc.
MEP Engineer: R Squared Consulting Engineers
Lighting Designer: Essential Light Design Studio
Food Service Consultant: Complete Restaurant Services
General Contractor: Arco Murray Design Build
Photography: Fredrik Brodén, Elizabeth Lavin
Artists/Artisans: Impressions Architectural Millwork, Springer Design Studio, Huy Nguyen

GOOD E

Dallas, Texas
Client: Westdale Real Estate Investment and Management
Droese Raney: David Droese, Reid Mulligan
Structural Engineer: Stenstrom-Schneider, Inc.
MEP Engineer: Purdy-McGuire, Inc.
Civil Engineer: Spiars Engineering
Landscape Architect: Kendall + Landscape Architecture
General Contractor: Andres Construction
Photography/Videography: Exploredinary

2800 MAIN

Dallas, Texas
Client: Westdale Real Estate Investment and Management
Droese Raney: Lance Raney, Reid Mulligan
Structural Engineer: Stenstrom-Schneider, Inc.
MEP Engineer: ARJO Engineers, Inc.
Civil Engineer: Kimley Horn
Landscape Architect: Kendall + Landscape Architecture
General Contractor: Verticon Construction (Harlowe), C1S Group, Inc. (base building)
Photography: Exploredinary

FORTY FIVE TEN

Dallas, Texas
Client: Headington Companies
Droese Raney: David Droese, Christine Howitt, Courtney Terrell
Architect of Record: Corgan
MEP Engineer: Blum Consulting Engineers, Inc.
Structural Engineer: Jaster-Quintanilla Engineering
Civil Engineer: Jaster-Quintanilla Engineering
Landscape Architect: Hocker
Lighting Designer: Essential Light Design Studio
Photography: Fredrik Brodén, Stephen Karlisch, Kurt Griesbach, Nathan Schroder
Artists/Artisans: Ceramica Suro, Larry Whitely, Impressions Architectural Millwork, Knoll, Jose Davila

THE WAREHOUSE

Dallas, Texas
Client: Howard Rachofsky
Droese Raney: David Droese, Reid Mulligan
MEP Engineer: ARJO Engineers, Inc.
Structural Engineer: Stenstrom-Schneider, Inc.
Lighting Designer: 2clighting
General Contractor: William C. Welch General Contractor
Photography: Exploredinary, Wade Griffith
Artists/Artisans: Texas Bomanite

THE CONSERVATORY

New York, New York; Dallas, Texas
Client: Brian Bolke
Droese Raney: David Droese, Christine Howitt
Architect of Record: Modus Architecture
MEP Engineer: Schnackel Engineers, Inc.
General Contractor: Petretti & Associates
Photography: David Marriott, Fredrik Brodén, Christine Howitt
Artists/Artisans: Larry Whitely, Impressions Architectural Millwork
Hand Renderings: Corvin Matei

JOSÉ

Dallas, Texas
Client: WoodHouse
Droese Raney: Lance Raney, Courtney Terrell
Structural Engineer: Stenstrom-Schneider, Inc.
MEP Engineer: ARJO Engineers, Inc.
Food Service Consultant: Consal Food Service Design
General Contractor: Rising Star Commercial
Photography: Steve Wrubel, Fredrik Brodén
Artists/Artisans: Ceramica Suro, Le Porc Shop, DMAC Construction

PERSONAL OFFICE

Dallas, Texas
Client: Private
Droese Raney: Lance Raney, Reid Mulligan
Structural Engineer: Stenstrom-Schneider, Inc.
MEP Engineer: Koegel Associates
Landscape Architect: Hocker
Interior Designer: Laura Kirar
General Contractor: Verticon Construction
Photography: Fredrik Brodén
Artists/Artisans: Orona, LM Fabrication

MI COCINA

Dallas, Texas
Client: MCrowd Restaurant Group
Droese Raney: Lance Raney, Christine Howitt, Courtney Terrell, Jonathan Mann, Heather Magee, Ricardo Torres
MEP Engineer: Schmidt & Stacy (Klyde Warren Park), McInnish Engineering (McKinney Ave.)
Structural Engineer: Stenstrom-Schneider, Inc.
Lighting Designer: Essential Light Design Studio (Klyde Warren Park), Byrdwaters Design (McKinney Ave.)
General Contractor: Maplewood Construction
Photography: Fredrik Brodén
Artists/Artisans: Luis Sotil, Impressions Architectural Millwork, Sarche Concrete Design, Sean Springer, Matthew Gilley Ceramics, Springer Design Studio, Orona, Cuellar Upholstery, Peter Glassford

ANGIE'S CONDO

Dallas, Texas
Client: Private
Droese Raney: Lance Raney
Lighting Design: Tully Weiss Lighting
General Contractor: Balfour Beatty
Photography: Steve Wrubel
Artists/Artisans: Teresita Fernandez, Dan Flavin, LM Fabrication

FLYING R RANCH

Goree, Texas
Client: Beth and Rob Rogers
Droese Raney: David Droese, Courtney Terrell
MEP Engineer: McInnish Engineering
Structural Engineer: Stenstrom-Schneider, Inc.
Lighting Design: Byrdwaters Design
General Contractor: Vista General Contractors, Inc.
Photography: Fredrik Brodén
Artists/Artisans: Wilson Live Edge, Alex Grazzini, David Weeks, Matthew Gilley Ceramics

RHEIMS RESIDENCE

Dallas, Texas
Client: Private
Droese Raney: David Droese
Landscape Architect: Hocker
Interior Designer: David Cadwallader
General Contractor: Travis and Travis
Photography: Fredrik Brodén
Artists/Artisans: Brad Oldham, LM Fabrication

GEISLER RESIDENCE

Dallas, Texas
Client: Stacey and Michael Geisler
Droese Raney: Lance Raney, Courtney Terrell
MEP Engineer: ARJO Engineers, Inc.
Structural Engineer: Stenstrom-Schneider, Inc.
General Contractor: Maplehill Residential, LLC, Tom Welker
Photography: Fredrik Brodén
Artists/Artisans: Jim and James Stevens

SYLVAN/POLLARD

Dallas, Texas
Client: Droese Raney
Droese Raney: David Droese, Lance Raney
MEP Engineer: ARJO Engineers, Inc.
Structural Engineer: Stenstrom-Schneider, Inc.
Photography: Fredrik Brodén
Artists/Artisans: LM Fabrication, Reid Mulligan, Adrian Orona, John Fife, Mike and Terry Millen, Lynn Penn, Impressions Architectural Millwork, Lance Satterfield

Current Droese Raney Team Members: David Droese, Lance Raney, Christine Howitt, Reid Mulligan, Rosana Avina, Courtney Terrell, Jonathan Mann, Heather Magee, Danielle Anderson, Matthew Gilley

Former Droese Raney Team Members: Adria Findley, Daniel Milligan, Madison Dahl, Ezra Loh, Ricardo Torres

ACKNOWLEDGMENTS

When we embarked on this project, we knew little about the process of writing a book. But we knew that we wanted to work with kindred spirits; with people who understood our practice; with collaborators aligned with our creative thinking. We found them and even took it a step further, making friends who feel more like family: Andrea Monfried, our ever-optimistic publishing consultant, who patiently guided us every step of the way (and whose automobile video conferences we will always treasure); Ian Volner, our writer, whose words so eloquently and beautifully convey our ethos (and who somehow remained the best-dressed person at breakfast no matter how far our travels took us); and Julie Savasky and Wendy Smith of Overstory, our designers, who told our story graphically and historically as no one else could (and whose strong opinions matched our own). Our meetings, dinners, and travels with this team felt like creative hangouts. We can't imagine going on this journey with anyone else.

We also express our gratitude to the architects, interior designers, artisans, and designers who have worked at Droese Raney since we started, as well as the countless engineers, landscape architects, consultants, and general contractors we've partnered with along the way. None of the projects in this book could have happened without your hard work, dedication, and talent.

Our biggest thanks go to our wonderful clients, the ones who have placed their trust in us and allowed us to bring their vision to reality with just a bit of Droese Raney flair. This book is for you.

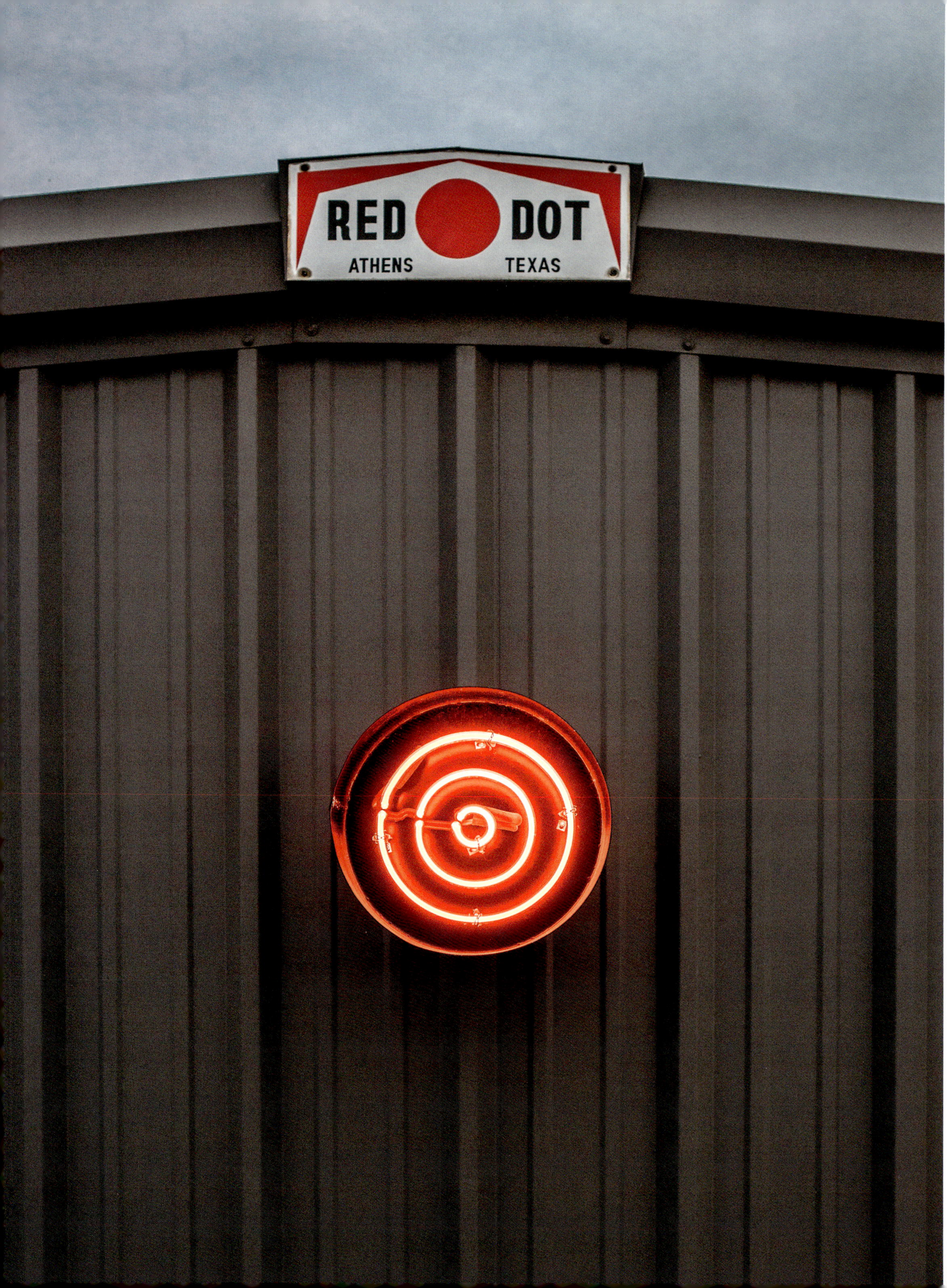
RED DOT
ATHENS TEXAS

Friends and Family

JOSÉ NOÉ SURO

I grew up in the ceramics workshop—all my school vacations were spent there, in the factory. Our company had been founded by my father in the 1950s; by the time I started a full-time job with him, in 1994, I had already started collecting art, and I told my father I wanted to invite artists to work in the factory as well. It was a very organic start, in a moment when contemporary art was completely different from what it is today: there was less interest, less money, more things to be discovered. That first generation of artists we collaborated with, most of them didn't even have a studio. So they used our factory. My father never thought that it was going to be a lot of artists, at least not all at the same time, and he was not pleased at first. He used to fire me every Friday and hire me again on Monday. But we really came to understand ceramics better through the eyes of the artists we were working with. They helped us to expand the boundaries of ceramics, because they saw the possibilities of the material, and how far you could go with it.

For me to work with an artist, I have to like what they're doing, and it's the same way with architects: I don't work with them unless I love their work. I've had people say about that approach "You're crazy; you're closing doors to some important people." But I think that it works in the opposite way: it's opened doors to work with other great people, people that I respect and admire, including some people who come knocking at the door, and it seems to me almost crazy that they're there. Droese Raney sort of showed up that way—they came to us while doing the Forty Five Ten project, and then before we knew it they were talking about wanting to open a Guadalajara-style tequila bar in Dallas. Crazy.

But I love Dallas, and I've made great friends there, the firm most of all. Guadalajara is my home, but Dallas is now the city where I spend the second largest amount of time. One of the only things I find problematic about Dallas is that, despite all the great art collections and great art institutions, so many artists struggle to stay there. They still haven't built their own scene, which I think is so important. We've become involved, partly through Droese Raney, with that cultural community, collaborating and collecting,

The work goes on: *Collaboration between Suro and Droese Raney usually means poring over materials and design ideas at Ceramica Suro in Guadalajara.*

Patterns and light: *The Dallas architects were sold on Suro's work—and friendship—the moment they saw the color and variety of his tiles.*

trying to show other people in Dallas that you don't have to be super rich to buy work by emerging artists. When I started out, I had no money; I was just creating these relationships, getting some work in exchange for giving people space and working together. And it's relationships like that that are the heart of generating a culturally vibrant place. We've been able to initiate a strong presence in Dallas, and already we're seeing a kind of mutual benefit and growth from that, with our artists in Guadalajara getting more exposure in the States and vice versa. The firm has been such a large factor in that.

Coming from Guadalajara, I'm a strong believer that individual efforts can change cities and places. For a lot of people of my generation, and my friends here who are involved with this place—chefs and artists and architects and myself—what we're doing in Guadalajara is working to change our community. It's been a very slow process, and a lot of personal effort has gone into it. But it's built on relationships. What I learned from my father, working with him in the summers, going to visit clients, was creating these bonds with clients: he always told me, "Your clients are the key to having a successful business; your clients have to become your friends." The bond that we've forged with Droese Raney, our traveling together and working together, the way it's become like a family: that's part of this community-building project, and together we've been able to bring that idea from Guadalajara to Dallas.

I feel lucky because, honestly, doing this kind of work is easy for me: it's easy whenever you're working with great people you really like and you have a natural connection with. If I'm going to work with a chef, I have to go to the restaurant and like the food, and when I'm working with a bar like Droese Raney—I mean, an office like Droese Raney! Not a bar! Although, seriously, you go to the Droese Raney office, you might have a tequila, and then you'll meet some kid there who's also an artist and who's working on a show: it's a different kind of architecture office than others I've seen, and it's what has made this such a productive partnership for us. Every project we work on with them, it's easy, whether it's a big department store like Forty Five Ten or a restaurant like José. Collaborators sometimes say to me, when they come to visit, "Oh, you're very generous." They're completely wrong; the truth is I'm super-selfish. I'm working with these architects and artists and artisans, getting them to come to Guadalajara, spending time with them, and introducing them to each other. And then I just sit back, learn, and enjoy myself. In one sense, I'm doing this for them, but I'm also doing it for me. Because, really, who doesn't want to spend time with their friends?

Forged in flames: *The deep color and textural glaze of the Guadalajaran tile brings a mesmerizing authenticity to Forty Five Ten, José restaurant, and other Droese Raney projects.*

The big show: *In 2023, the Dallas Contemporary devoted a major exhibition to Suro's collection as well as to works from Ceramica Suro. Naturally, Droese Raney had a hand in putting the show together, giving their old friend a hearty Texas welcome.*

COLLABORATION

The Extra Mile

HOWARD RACHOFSKY

The original idea behind the Warehouse was as much pragmatic as it was artistic. We had a collection that had been building for, at that time, fifteen years. We had a lot of art, and we were spending a fortune on art storage. You know, it's wonderful when you can exhibit art, but it's not so wonderful when you have to have it all packed up in crates, and every time you go to visit it you have to pull it out and move it around. It's a real production. So we got the idea of doing a little space, ideally a small exhibition space and reading room and then a somewhat larger deep storage space where we could keep the collection.

We had to run some numbers and exert some degree of pragmatism. Fortunately, when we started down this path, a good friend of mine—the late Vernon Faulconer, who was a Dallas Museum trustee and a great collector himself—said he'd like to partner with us. We started looking at spaces together, looking at a few buildings. Mostly we struck out. Finally, we stumbled on what turned out to be a pretty wonderful property in a really accessible location, literally ten minutes from our house by the highway, and with a huge potential audience surrounding it. So we bought this building. It was an old tilt-wall building, really nothing to it, just a former Aaron's furniture warehouse and showroom on a little two-acre site. Essentially what we had was an empty vessel, and we had to figure out what we were going to do with it.

It was at that point that we teamed up with Allan Schwartzman, one of the best art advisors out there. We traveled all over the world trying to see examples of what to do and what not to do with a space like this. Frankly, we looked like complete idiots: there we are in these European exhibition spaces, trying to get a sense of scale by pacing off exhibition rooms, going step by step to measure them, all the security guards watching us like we're crazy. But the whole time we were really thinking about the experience of the art. What we wanted to build, basically, was a laboratory.

That's what Droese Raney gave us in the end. But not just that. What they've built is a space with this extraordinary kind of light, with the best possible functional aspects for showing art, and all

Different artists, different scales: *For the Warehouse, Droese Raney explored various museological conditions, using models to frame the visitor experience.*

Research into results: *The flexible, ever-changing plan of the Warehouse gives the Rachofsky Collection room to breathe. The spatial narrative carries through from gallery to art-packed gallery.*

within the practical constraints we'd established at the outset. You think about these other big institutions that spend hundreds of millions of dollars on their buildings, when really that should be spent on the art. What we got was something every bit as effective as one of those supposedly more elaborate structures, but with the focus less on the building and more on the work. As I look back now, darn close to a decade later, there are not a whole lot of things that I would change. It's really stood the test of time.

My first instructions to Droese Raney were, basically, Don't mess this up. One of the signature points, for me, is that in so many other museum spaces, the first few rooms are homogeneous and not that interesting, making you feel sort of fatigued by the time you get through them. What we did here with Droese Raney was to modulate the scale of the spaces in a way that keeps it stimulating. You enjoy being in the space you're in, but then you also look forward to going to the next space, and then the next and the next. Nothing looks exactly like the space you just left. You're always feeling yourself becoming a little more oriented within the overall environment, but also a little disoriented at the same time; you're given the opportunity to engage with the art on your own terms. And this sort of subtle manipulation has consistently worked with every exhibition we've done there over the years. Working alongside Allan, who's also helped us find curators to bring in fresh perspectives, we've seen how each person we collaborate with is able to attack the spaces in a completely different way—as though the spaces were perfectly happy to get a different look, a different spin.

A project like this works best when everybody is engaged, checks their ego at the door, and pulls together to create a consensus. I always hark back to the belief that the building has to let the art be the art, to multiply the value of the artistic encounter, which is something that I think is not always well understood or well accepted elsewhere in architecture or in the art world. Being conscious of that value and putting it first: that's pretty meaningful. That's at the core of this project, and that's what David, Lance, and the team realized from the start. They know art, and I think the things they've done since, working directly with artists, really show that.

When we were putting together a sculpture by the artist Nobuo Sekine—kind of a giant rock on a huge column—it was the Droese Raney folks who went the extra mile, found a quarry, picked out this big pink potato-looking rock, then got the artist's approval and helped us to set up. That level of commitment, that's what moved me from not quite understanding what the firm was about to eventually feeling confident enough with them to bring them on board to renovate my house. It was all the things they saw that, frankly, the rest of us didn't see right away. Take that cove lighting in the Warehouse library. That was David's idea. At first we thought, Well, maybe that's something we'll have to sacrifice. But in the end we didn't, and it's really quite beautiful. Sometimes you have to choose this or that, but occasionally you can have both—it's always a matter of choices. I'm just glad we made the right ones.

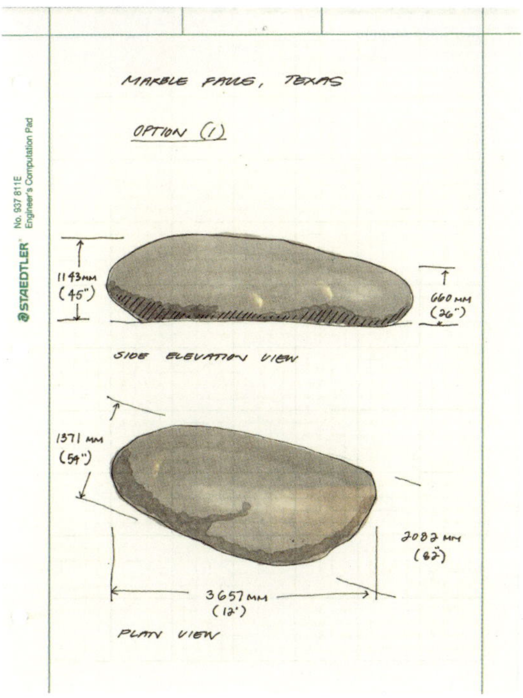

Between a rock and a hard place: *After the success of the Warehouse, the architects and their client teamed up on a one-of-a-kind installation by artist Nobuo Sekine on the grounds of the Rachofsky House.*

Illuminated manuscripts: *Concealed fluorescent fixtures in the Warehouse library weren't a part of the original scheme. But with a little persuading from his architects, Rachofsky eventually saw the light.*

Warp and Weft

DOROTHY COSONAS

During my tenure as creative director of KnollTextiles, there were only a few projects that really stood out. I mean, I've been involved with a lot of top-level ideas and concepts; some happened, some didn't. But I've always looked at Forty Five Ten as being right up there with some of the best work we did: it's on par with the TWA Hotel in New York, for example, or when I worked with Apple. It was the level of involvement and interaction—both with Forty Five Ten's founder Brian Bolke and with Droese Raney—that really allowed us to feel important as a brand. I mean, for someone to look at Knoll textiles and say, "Great, we want it for the *entire concept*," that's just really unusual. Typically budgets start happening and other people have their opinions and eventually you expect someone to say "Why just one company?" And it turned out to be a huge opportunity for us to create a range of different new products, allowing us to be seen in a different way. It was also the last project of this scale that Knoll did before the company merged with Herman Miller, so in that sense it's become a part of the legacy of the brand.

It all started pretty randomly. Droese Raney reached out to us at Knoll, to furniture and textiles; as they explained it to me, they were doing this high-end fashion store in Dallas, working with Brian Bolke, and they were wondering what would happen if they tried using Knoll for the whole project. I think it was almost intended as a joke, but they decided to see if it was possible. And as soon as I heard that, I thought, I'm in. I just immediately felt very connected to it. It's not like I was ever not engaged with our projects; it's just that frequently my salespeople would handle the particulars and I would find myself kept at some distance. But with Forty Five Ten, I was totally engaged. I felt like every detail needed to be fully thought through from our end. This idea of taking our products, and then adjusting them to Droese Raney's vision, seeing how far we could push them—it was something else. We were deploying the design language we were so familiar with but reinterpreting it specifically for Forty Five Ten.

Obviously, I loved that Droese Raney decided to stick with us, taking an all-Knoll approach to the interior. But what was really

New directions: *Florence Knoll made her namesake company a veritable byword for modernist purity and authenticity. Cosonas's collaboration with Droese Raney built on that tradition and at the same time took Forty Five Ten into uncharted, eye-popping terrain.*

Luxe, calme, volupté: *The designers upended expectations (and surprised even the seasoned Cosonas) by finding new applications for some of Knoll's iconic designs: patterned fabric on mannequins, famous chairs in unfamiliar upholstery.*

extraordinary, I thought, was the way the firm used our products and materials while going way beyond what was expected. There were so many surprises: having the fabrics live on the mannequins; having the fabrics live within the accessories; the amazing drapery in the shoe department. When you see something like the Eclat Weave—an Anni Albers fabric from the 1970s, which usually goes on a chair or a sofa—made into these wonderful sorts of cacti forms within the space, it's just very exciting. There was so much customization, too, redoing some of our tables in rose gold, changing leg heights, putting very inexpensive upholsteries in unexpected places, like on some very expensive furniture by David Adjaye. They even used a textile that I had derived from the pattern on a rug belonging to my grandmother: something very meaningful to me and not something I ever thought I'd see in a fancy department store! Again and again, I just thought to myself, Wow, I could never have thought of that.

That attention to detail really helped the company to think about textiles in a different way, opening the doors to different types of projects and working with different types of clients. It helped us especially to move forward in a new way with residential work—there were some very beautiful houses that we got involved in after that. It's too bad we weren't able to photograph them, because they were private homes, but it just felt good knowing that these products were living in someone's penthouse or their summer cottage or whatever. Those weren't the kinds of spaces we were really in before; there are so many other home decor brands out there, some of them maybe more conventionally domestic, as opposed to Knoll's more modernist edge. Knowing that our work could be in those kinds of environments, I was just over the moon, like, Oh, someone chose us! The project got a huge amount of press, and we capitalized on that, putting some of the custom pieces in our showrooms and on the website, spotlighting this new dimension for the brand. Forty Five Ten showed we had something that could appeal to a specific kind of client who was looking for luxury and comfort.

And that goes right back to the original concept. From the beginning, I always looked at Forty Five Ten not just as a place to buy clothes but as an *experience*, a place that you really desired to go. I think that's what we were so successful in doing, creating an ambience that people are drawn to and then want to stay in for a long time. From the very moment the customers walk in, with the mannequins placed by the door, it's like, Okay, here we are, Dallas! Come on in. It takes a special kind of team to create that effect. I mean, I've dealt with a lot of people in my time, and you get a rather varying range of interest and dedication to what the end result should be. With this project, the dedication never wavered. The firm just said, "This is what we'd like, this is what we want to do, let's figure out how to get there." And Brian was game to go wherever that process led. I was just thrilled to be a part of that ride.

To me, good design is lasting design. When you look at something and you can't place a date on it, that to me is where good design comes into play. It's really about walking into an interior and feeling either a sense of calm or excitement or something that prompts an emotion and that keeps doing so, that still feels that way as time goes by. That can be awfully tricky, but Forty Five Ten has managed it: here we are, years later, and it's still a space that makes people feel somehow important just to be there. You know you're not in any old average location; you know you're in a space people have thought hard about. That's the thing about design. You can sense—you *have* to be able to sense—when someone has thought about how a space should be. It's a rare thing to find.

Group effort: *The success of Forty Five Ten was an all-hands affair. Client Brian Bolke, Droese Raney's Courtney Terrell and Christine Howitt, and Cosonas, here at the Knoll corporate offices in New York, were part of the team that minded every detail.*

The gang's all here: *The opening of Forty Five Ten saw Bolke, Terrell, Raney, Howitt, Cosonas, and Droese in festive attire. The Droese Raney team sported jackets made from a Cosonas-designed textile, one inspired by a treasured rug that had belonged to her grandmother.*